THE LI

YORKSHIRE LAD

Born near Doncaster

Gordon Frederick Coggon

First printing: 2020

ISBN: 9798574845400
Also available for Kindle from Amazon

All profits from this book will be donated to LABRATS International, to support the work of individuals and organisations representing the atomic and nuclear test communities across the world.

LABRATS (Legacy of the Atomic Bomb. Recognition for Atomic Test Survivors) CIC, company number 12874772.

CHAPTER ONE

My life began in a nursing home on the 24th November 1938. I was the first son of a farmer, Frederick Coggon, who worked land on Bridge Farm in Epworth Turbary, which lies just on the South Yorkshire border between Doncaster and Scunthorpe. I caught both German measles and the ordinary type of measles at the nursing home. While recovering from those two illnesses, I was diagnosed with two abscesses in my neck, but I was initially too weak to have the operation to remove them.

This complication resulted in me staying in hospital until I was one year and five months old. In fact, my mum gave birth to my sister before I went home.

The war started just after I came home, and things were very hard for people. Food and clothing were increasingly scarce and rationing of food made things even more arduous.

German prisoners of war came from Sandtoft prison camp to work on our land, and one of them used to have dinner with us sometimes. I remember him well. His name was Otto, and he made my sister a ring out of a silver thruppenny bit. But most of all I remember the Lancaster model he made for me from matchsticks and sugar bag paper. Otto was a pilot who was shot down and captured. He didn't like bombing people, but, like our own pilots, he had to do his duty.

One day, when I was about five years old, I found what I thought was part of an aircraft. My pal from a neighbouring house and I soon got curious and tried to open it by hitting it with Dad's kindling hatchet to see what was rattling inside. We were making a lot of noise. Mum saw what we were doing and told us to go indoors and leave the thing where it was. Dad came out to see what we had found and immediately went off to fetch someone else, who told us how lucky we were not to have been killed because it was an incendiary bomb! They were being dropped in great numbers all over the place, probably to set fire to our corn stacks. Another day, I remember a Luftwaffe fighter plane strafing the Land Army girls in one of our fields.

We used to collect the rolls of silver paper dropped from aircraft to block radar, and 'aeroplane glass' was a jewel for us young ones. This was the window material from crashed aircraft, which you could put holes through with a hot poker. It was, in fact, a kind of Perspex or plastic, which wasn't readily available to buy at the time, but of course it was a real party piece to actually burn a hole through a piece of glass and we often traded it at school for sweets or what have you.

In the winter of 1947, which was recorded as the worst winter in British history, our farm and four neighbouring farms were flooded after snowfall when drifts up to seven feet high started to melt in June. Then the flooded land froze, and the fields were turned to ice too. People came from all over to skate on them.

Consequently, my father lost his entire winter wheat crop and the land was unfit to grow anything for the next year.

This led to my dad nearly losing his farm with all the seed bills and fertilizer bills owing and wages to pay, along with cattle and other stock to feed. It almost bankrupted him, but with help from his brother, who had a farm in Doncaster, he managed to keep the farm going for another four years. My other uncle, who owned the farm next to ours, eventually lost his farm to the floods, and our neighbouring farmers did too.

Threshing Day, an oil painting by G F Coggon

The Farm Worker

Winter bites with a hungry greed
Upon a man with mouths to feed,
Driving snow on his face is fanned
To daunt the worker of the land.
From early morn to late at night
He toils a weary eternal fight
Against an element of bitter cold,
Protector of seeds; no weeds enfold.

Summer comes with blistering heat
Upon a man with harvest to reap,
Sweating; boiling; choking dust
Never stopping, for work he must.
Outrun the summer's relentless race
To gather seed and eventually face,
An autumn planting, sowing grain,
And the icy fingers of winter again.

GF Coggon, 1994

CHAPTER TWO

As a teenager I attended Haxey School, which is approximately five miles south of Epworth. My parents bought a smallholding nearby and Dad worked on a farm near our new home.

I left school at the age of fifteen. In those days, the education authority would give you some choices of employment according to your academic qualifications. I was given a few options, from which I chose deep sea fishing. So off I went to the Port of Grimsby, where I reported to the Deep Sea Fishing Academy. They kitted me out with a cape and leggings, sou'wester, two pairs of sea boot socks and a couple of woolly jumpers, plus a pair of wellingtons.

The following morning, after spending the night at the Deep Sea Mission, I reported as instructed to the North Sea trawler *Ampulla*. I introduced myself but the crew seemed very doubtful that I would settle into the life of a trawler man. They explained that eighty per cent of the men who came to the job from the country life of farming did not like life at sea. I, being a mere lad of fifteen, was sure that I would, but that was my youthful eagerness trying to impress.

My opening task aboard was down in the boiler room, where I had my first encounter with the job of chipping coal. It entailed breaking large lumps of coal with a 12-pound hammer and shovelling them into a barrow, then wheeling it to the stoker, who fed it with a shovel into the furnace. This I carried out for about an hour before I went up to the galley for a drink. It was hard work and I had stripped to the waist, it was so hot down there.

At 07.45 we started to move away from the quayside amid belching smoke from the funnel; it was a refreshing smell, like steam trains. There must have been a lot of trawlers moving out to sea because the skippers were sounding their steam horns at each other.

The North Sea was very choppy, with white capped waves and seagulls darting around the ship. The cormorants were really fascinating to watch as they closed their wings in mid-air and dived into the sea from heights of fifty feet or more, very rarely coming to the surface without a fish. While watching these birds I was very sea sick – and we were only just out of the Humber estuary.

My next job was mending nets. I was given a pointed shuttle needle, ten inches by four inches, which was loaded with twine, and I was shown how to make new squares in nets that were broken. This task was done in-between going to the side of the ship to be sick. This sickness was with me, on and off, for the entire three weeks I was on board the vessel.

The very first time I was involved in actual trawling was a real education. We were woken by the ship's horn and the rumbling of the steam winch hauling the nets in. We all got on deck quickly, and I was told to do this and that until the net, complete with buoys and rollers, was lifted, along with two big wooden platform affairs. There must have been about a ton of fish emptied onto the deck after one of the crew undid the 'cod end', which is the far end of the net where the fish are trapped. When it was released we were up to our wellington tops in fish of various types and sizes, all wriggling and flapping about around our feet. First, we had to throw overboard the tiny fish that had not escaped the net. Then, using a gutting knife, I was shown how to take out the intestines of the fish and throw them into the waste buckets, then place the finished fish in boxes to be taken to the cold room and packed in ice. The whole process, from taking out the nets to putting them overboard again, took about two and a half hours. During this time the gulls were having a field day, even trying to grab fish out of our hands, but mainly after the waste that was thrown overboard. This procedure was repeated about four hours after the nets went back in the sea, day and night. It was real graft.

The second week out in the North Sea was terrifying as we were caught in a force nine. The skipper had ordered the nets to be pulled aboard earlier and warned me, being a young inexperienced lad, to take special care and not go on deck unless absolutely necessary, and only then if I had someone with experience with me. As it happened, I had to go to the toilet and was shown how to get there safely in the gale. There were rope guidelines strung between the different super structures so, by timing my passage and holding on, I managed to reach the toilet near the stern of the ship. I had just got comfortable when a massive wave came through the half-open door and almost drowned me. I near enough ran back to the crew quarters, where the other men made a few jokes about me getting washed out of the 'karzey'. The waves were like sitting on the top of a mountain one minute and looking up the side of a mountain the next. I was terrified we were all going to drown.

My first impressions of the 'mate' of the vessel had been unimpressive because he seemed a miserable sort of person, but later I found him to be an okay kind of guy. Whilst taking a turn on watch on the bridge, he showed me the echo sounding equipment and the paper graph it printed of the sea bottom and patiently told me what 'this and that' was used for. He let me turn the rudder wheel when the four bells sounded, which was the signal to alter course and put the ship on a different heading – all under his supervision, of course, and once the weather had subsided to a steady swell.

On the Friday of our third week out on the North Sea, the skipper told us we were on our way back to port; we had filled our kit of fish despite the storm holding things up for almost a day and a night. We arrived back at Grimsby that afternoon and I bade my farewell to everyone. I could not wait to get home.

Grimsby Trawler Ampulla GY 949

CHAPTER THREE

When I arrived home, I started a job on the farm where my father worked, working with shire horses in differing capacities. However, it was hard work for very low pay and eventually I and a friend who also worked there decided to look for something else.

An advertisement in the local paper, *The Doncaster Evening News,* announced that a Nottingham firm that did shaft sinking and drilling was offering employment on a drilling platform on Gringley Hill, about five miles from my home. My friend and I applied for jobs there and were accepted as 'spanner men' – but first we had to build the derrick, which was a wooden structure a hundred and twenty feet tall, covered with slatted walls with open windows on each storey.

After the structure had been made, the heavy diesel engine had to be manhandled on rollers into position and bolted down to the concrete floor. Then the winch and the drilling platform were erected.

Spanner men' were given the name because that is what they used. As the hollow eighty-foot threaded pipes were lowered into the drilled hole, a steel scissor clamp was placed across the steel-cased hole, going under the threaded knuckle joint of the last of the joined pipes, and was held there. The spanner men would use long levered spanners to screw or unscrew the pipes together or apart, as required. The scissors stopped the pipes that were already screwed together from falling down the hole and being lost.

Not long after we started, the shift system changed and instead of working three shifts, we were split into four shifts. My friend was promoted to 'winch man' and I became 'top man'. The winch man was next in line to the shift foreman and he was responsible for the actual drilling of the hole, which included lifting the pipes out of the hole one by one until up to seventy eighty-foot pipes were laid out on a table made of wood similar to railway sleepers. The last pipe out of the hole wasn't in fact a pipe but a ten-inch diameter tube about twenty feet long with a screw-on type of industrial diamond bit at the bottom. This was also hollow and allowed the core of different strata of rock to pass into the tube; this would be emptied onto a suitable area of ground outside in lines and in the order that it was drilled, so the site manager, who was a geologist, could examine the rock we had drilled through. My role as 'top man' was to stand on a scaffold plank eighty feet above the winch and undo the pin that secured a collar around the knuckle of each eighty feet of pipe as it was hauled up and unscrewed. Just as it was placed on the table the weight of the pipe would slacken the strain and allow me to pull the lifting chair away from the pipe. The winch man then lowered the chair with the locking pin undone to bring up another pipe out of the hole or to lower one down, whichever the case may be.

In between the drilling we had to carry out other tasks, like mixing the Bentonite, a liquid that was pumped down the hole to swill out the swarf from the drill and lubricate the drill bit. We also had to screw together casing that was lowered into the hole if it was likely to collapse in on itself. These casings were wide at the top of the hole but gradually got smaller the deeper they went, and, in turn, the drill size would decrease as the hole shrunk in size. There were not many other tasks, except to keep the tea flowing, especially for the winch man who was at his post all the time that the drilling was taking place. We also had to keep the diesel tank full on the big engine.

Every week I gave my mother my wages and she gave me pocket money. By this time, I had five brothers and five sisters, four of whom were already working. I earned almost twice as much in wages as my father did. However, the farm work had its advantages, and we always had plenty of vegetables and milk free of charge.

Most weekends I would catch a Lincolnshire road car bus into Doncaster bus station, which was then called Glasgow Paddocks, and go to watch films at the Gaumont, Esseldo, Ritz or Regal. Sadly, these beautiful old picture houses have long since disappeared and been taken over by multiscreen venues on urban sites.

We found two seams of coal and had drilled down about one thousand five hundred feet by the time I was called up for National Service.

CHAPTER FOUR

After registering at the recruiting office in Doncaster, I had to go to RAF Cardington in Bedfordshire to collect my RAF kit and have my medical. The next stage was to proceed to RAF Padgate, near Warrington, for my basic training.

When I signed on at the recruiting office in Doncaster, I was convinced by the Recruiting Officer that instead of doing two and a half years of National Service, I would be able to join the RAF if I was prepared to sign on as a regular airman for a period of three years. It would give me a better wage and also, if at a later stage in my service I decided to sign on for a longer period, I would be offered a wider choice of trades. For my initial three years' service there were limited trades available and I picked one described as 'Administrative Orderly', which I later realised was just a fancy name for 'jack of all trades but master of none.'

On arrival at RAF Padgate, after all the administrative tasks were done, I collected my bedding and was allocated a billet. This was a term used in the forces in those days to describe one's living quarters if you were a single person. If you were married, you could apply for a 'married quarter'.

Corporal Short was the drill instructor who was in charge of our Flight. He lived at the end of our billet in a single bunk, and he made it quite clear that he didn't like anyone; he would go out of his way to make life uncomfortable and almost unbearable. There were twenty new recruits and we all resided in the same room, which was long and had ten bed spaces along each side. The middle of the floor was unoccupied except for a pot-bellied black stove that burnt coke. When lit it kept the room quite warm, sometimes uncomfortably so if it was kindled with too much coke, when the belly of the stove would glow red hot. Next to the stove was the coke bin, which was a two-handled affair. When it needed refilling, two of us recruits were detailed to take it to the coke store yard, which was about half a mile from our billet. After we had trudged there and back, slipping and sliding in the snow with our heavy burden, Corporal Short made us go back with his bin and refill that.

On our first morning at RAF Padgate we were rudely awakened by the Orderly Sergeant who came into the billet, tipped the bed clothes off us and shouted for everyone to get out of bed and stand to attention. It was 06.30 hours. The duties of Orderly Sergeant and Orderly Officer in the RAF were set down in the Station Standing Orders and it was a chargeable offence for anyone not to read them. The day to day running of a RAF station depended on orders of one kind or another.

The next eight weeks were filled with drills known as 'square bashing.' Normally square bashing was only practised for four weeks but RAF Padgate was closing down as a training centre and the four extra weeks of drill was ordered because the passing out parade was going to be televised.

Corporal Short gave me extra duties by making me the person who rekindled his stove every morning, ready to light again at night. I would have to take out all the ashes, lay paper and wood in the stove and then 'black lead' it, which kept the stove looking like new.

At last, the day came when we were to pass out on the parade ground. We were all dressed in our best blue uniforms, ready to do our drills in front of the television cameras; some of the recruits' families were also there watching.

As soon as we finished the parade, we would be on our way home on leave, equipped with our new posting instructions, which we had been given the night before. My posting was to RAF Hemswell, near Lincoln. That morning, after I laid the stove for Corporal 'Hitler' Short, instead of black leading it I polished it with boot polish, knowing he would be staying there for at least another couple of weeks.

During the parade the order came to "Slope, order and present arms." As I took my 303 rifle off my shoulder, the safety catch got stuck on my greatcoat button, which went flying across the parade ground. Luck was with me because no one noticed.

CHAPTER FIVE

After my two weeks' leave ended, I travelled to RAF Hemswell, which is near Lincoln and only 15 miles from my home, where I had spent my leave.

Once I was settled there, I was given employment as an Aircraft Assistant in the orderly room of 199 Squadron, which was a Lincoln bomber squadron situated in number four hangar. A Flight Sergeant and a Corporal were also based there. My work entailed general duties like typing addresses on envelopes, checking leave applications, amending Queen's regulations and lighting a stove in one of the many offices down each side of the hangar.

I enjoyed my short stay at Hemswell, during which I took flights in a Lincoln bomber whenever I could. It was during my first flight that I had an accident with my parachute, which I was required to have with me. The Chief (Flt/Sgt) loaned me his bicycle to go and fetch my parachute from the safety equipment section. On the way back, whilst trying to adjust it under my arm, I accidentally pulled the rip cord and, to make matters worse, it got caught up in the bike chain. I wasn't the most popular guy in the Safety Equipment Officer's opinion. I will say no more on the subject.

I regained a lot of my credibility when I joined the

squadron boxing team. It was a sport I had enjoyed since leaving school, when I had joined a boxing club in Doncaster, and I was good at it. During those few months at Hemswell I was flown to the Lord Wakefield's Amateur Championship Trophy and took part in the light heavyweight bouts, which I won. Then I went to Fontainebleau in France to box in the British Allied Forces in Europe Championships. Then came more exhibition fights. However, it all came to an end when, during training, the spring punch bag assembly hit me in the face and broke my nose very badly. I ended up in Nocton Hall RAF Hospital where they put a plate in my nose, finishing my boxing career.

In August 1957 I received my next posting. It was to a tropical Pacific atoll two degrees off the equator, called Christmas Island.

*My oil painting of the Battle of Britain Flight,
which, many years later, was stationed at Scampton,
just up the road from Hemswell.*

CHAPTER SIX

I had a couple of weeks' embarkation leave and then went to RAF Cardington to collect my tropical clothing: khaki drill shorts, socks, shirts and longs, plus a pair of aircrew sunglasses. The next stop was London Heathrow Airport, where I was to fly by BOAC Stratocruiser, second class. I made friends with a group of other airmen, one of whom later became my best mate.

The journey would entail flying to Gander in Canada, then on to New York, where we stayed the night in the Governor Clinton Motel.

The highways over there were awesome: six lanes of traffic on each side of the road, and roundabouts stacked up to four high with loads of roads at different levels. In the hotel we each had a single room, each with a colour television with loads of channels to pick from. Most of us had never seen colour television before; in fact, I had only seen black and white TV in a neighbour's house before I joined the forces because we didn't have an electricity supply in our house. We had to use paraffin lamps – either the ones with wicks or the pump-up Tilly lamps. Even the toilet system wasn't connected to a sewer; it was the septic tank type.

Four of us went downtown for a look round and a lager, it

was amazing how everything was so different to what we were used to.

We took off from New York in a Trans American Airways Super Constellation. This was a fantastic experience because we were flying in broad daylight across the States, east to west to San Francisco, seeing places I had read about in Westerns, a lot of names that I remembered. There was Lake Michigan and Lake Erie, Chicago, and Las Vegas. Flying over Salt Lake City fooled me though. As I looked down, I said, "It's snowing down there." Everything was white, but it turned out that it was the salt lake that I was looking at. We were served a salad with little pieces of toast and caviar – I don't know what all the fuss is about with that. All those rich people paying enormous prices for fish eggs? It tastes disgusting.

The weather was very warm when we landed at San Francisco, but not uncomfortably so. The four of us who had made friends decided it was too good an opportunity to miss so we went on another sightseeing tour. The Golden Gate Bridge was a fantastic sight, and, in the distance, we could see what I was told was the prison island of Alcatraz.

Right from the start of our stay in the USA I noticed that cars were driven without much care of distancing between vehicles; twice I saw multiple slight bumps when the cars pulled up at lights and concertinaed into each other. Instead of exchanging details they just swore at each other, waved their arms and then set off again. You could actually hear their bumpers clanging each other! If that had happened at home, there would have been a traffic jam on the road whilst drivers exchanged insurance details. We asked our taxi driver about this and he just shrugged his shoulders, smiled, and lifted both hands in a relaxed, unbothered attitude.

We visited a diner and had waffles and coffee, which was really nice. I remember my mum making something like waffles in a pair of iron-jawed tongs, which had sections squared off in a shape like a bar of chocolate. She would fill them with a batter-like substance, then put the tongs in the hot coals and the end result would be something resembling the waffles we had just eaten.

The visit seemed far too short and we set off again in the early morning light, this time heading for Hawaii. The journey was filled with conversation and postcard writing because the view out of the window was just the Pacific Ocean in all directions.

There was quite a bit of excitement when the islands of Hawaii came into view, first the mountains and then green palm trees and white surf on golden sands.

Our hosts were the United States Air Force at their base at Hickham Field. It looked typically American, with many varied aircraft parked all over the base, but one could not wish for better hosts. The food in their multi-ranked canteen was exotic and delicious as well as plentiful. Something I found odd though was that their toilet cubicles had no doors; they were in rows and men sat in full view of anyone going in.

We were to remain at USAF Hickham for four days, during which time we explored many places I had heard of, like the sunken battleship *Arizona* which was left as a tomb for all the lives lost when the Japanese attacked Pearl Harbour during the Second World War.

We visited the outskirts of the city, which I found to be quite different. The people were hard-working and seemed a lot poorer than their counterparts in the built-up areas where tourism afforded a better lifestyle, I guessed.

We all bought fancy Hawaiian t-shirts and shorts and I also bought three pairs of rubber slippers with straps on the front that enabled one to put one's toes between the straps to keep them on. Of course, we now know them as flip-flops.

All too soon we were on our way again. This time we boarded an RAF Transport aircraft called a Hastings; this was a four-engine turboprop that was soon to be replaced with the more modern Britannia Transporter Aircraft.

We took off, then turned back again because of a problem. A reprieve! It allowed us another two days to explore the islands. This was taken advantage of to the full and by the time we were on our way again we had managed to do some more shopping. I bought my mum a Hawaiian necklace, which was silver and hand-crafted in the South Sea Island style. This and our postcards were all sent home before we continued our journey.

Flying in the unpressurised Hastings was very uncomfortable and cold compared with the civilian airliners. The noise was that loud you had to shout to make yourself heard. It's roughly one thousand eight hundred miles from Hawaii to Christmas Island, which is only two degrees off the equator and part of the Marshall Islands.

As we began to lose height, noted by a sudden change of engine noise and the feeling of ears popping, the island came into view. From where we were sitting it looked to be more water than land, but as we lost altitude and approached the runway, it became clear the island was split up by many lagoons.

CHAPTER SEVEN

The long journey from Heathrow had finally ended – and didn't we know it! By the time our baggage was on board the three-tonne lorry sent to collect us we were sweating. Everything we did seemed like hard work and made us wringing wet with sweat. Later on, we would become acclimatised to the hot humid weather.

Our transport continued along a bumpy track, amid coconut trees and the blinding vision of white coral interrupted by occasional tropical bushes of some kind or another. About ten minutes after we set off, we arrived at what was called Main Camp, its name derived from the obvious, because there must have been at least two hundred tents of various sizes and shapes and in two colours, green and white.

The real names of people are not mentioned in this book to avoid embarrassment or upset at a later date; this is necessary because a lot of people I knew back then have now passed on.

My friend – whom I shall name Dusty Miller – and I were shown into a white four-man tent. Outside was a board with the words "Tent 222 – enter at your own peril." We had noticed earlier that large land crabs were roaming around everywhere, and some tents had crabs tied with string to the guy ropes.

The tent was already occupied because there were only two empty spaces. The other occupants were presumably still at work, but their belongings were stowed in cardboard boxes beside their camp beds.

Dusty and I dumped our kit in the tent and went off to find the bedding store. The corporal in there told us we must go to the headquarters' tent first and book in, which we did. Then we went on to various sections of trade to get signatures on the blue card we had been given. This procedure wasn't another unnecessary discipline; in fact, it was a very sound idea, as the purpose of getting the signatures was a practical way of making sure all the equipment that one was loaned from a particular station would be returned to that place of borrowing. If you did not get a signature on return, then you paid for the equipment you had lost out of your wages. One of the signatures was to be signed by the bedding store NCO in charge. The bedding comprised of three blankets (it got very cold at night), two sheets, two pillows and slips, one mosquito net and one camp bed, plus an oblong meal tray complete with knife, fork, spoon and mug. The tray had indents to hold a dinner in one section, a place for a sweet and one for soup or your mug, whichever you preferred. If you required both you went back for your cup to be filled with tea or coffee.

We carried our bundles back to the tent, thankful we had remembered where it was because everywhere looked the same. Every few paces we were confronted with large crabs and Dusty said he wasn't sleeping next to the floor with those ugly critters creeping in bed with him.

So, after the job of putting the camp beds together, we

decided to look for some timber to make a suitable stage to raise them higher than the normal six inches they stood off the sandy floor. We went to the REME workshops, where there was a scrapheap full of offcut pieces of wood and pallets, and we were told to help ourselves. Later, after scrounging other bits and pieces such as a saw and nails and borrowing a hammer (which was in fact the flat end of a small axe), we managed to build a couple of raised stages for our beds. We later made other furniture to stow our gear in. We introduced ourselves to the other chaps who occupied the tent and they said they were cooks in the Sergeants' Mess. This turned out to be great because we could always go and make ourselves a sandwich in their kitchen.

The following day we both reported to the Station Warrant Officer to be put to work. For the first three weeks we were put on tent erection duties. This was hard work, especially with the larger marquees, and usually we could not wait to have a cold shower in water from the distillery plant that adequately supplied the whole of Main Camp. The water was sourced from the ocean and distilled using a ship's boiler run by an old petty officer and his crew. There was also lots of bottled water available for drinking.

The next task we were made to do was not for the weak-hearted. We were on the sewage detail, mostly undertaken by individuals who were available at the time and not a permanent duty for anyone. This job was to empty the hessian-covered toilets by taking out the bucket under the seat and emptying it into the sewage lorry, which was driven by Dusty sometimes (although mostly he was transporting troops here and there). Then we had to put blue disinfectant in the empty bucket before putting it back in the toilet. Most of the camp had to take their turn but it was a smelly, horrible task.

CHAPTER EIGHT

It was now November 1957 and we had been told when we arrived on Christmas Island that we were here to prepare the accommodation for the testing of nuclear bombs. Tests had already been conducted at Malden Island, and the next test in the present series of Operation Grapple was to be here at Christmas Island. Loudspeakers had been erected all around the camp and they announced that the next test was imminent; called Grapple X, it would be dropped 20 miles from the island by a Valiant 'V' bomber. In the meantime, we were given two dummy run exercises using the aircraft involved and everyone on the island. There would be Shackleton search and rescue aircraft to make sure no shipping was in the Ground Zero area, and Canberra sample aircraft would fly through the bomb cloud to collect radiation data.

The manpower consisted of about 2000 to 3000 troops from Great Britain and the Commonwealth troops of Fiji, New Zealand, Australia and others. There were also the local inhabitants, the Gilbertese Islanders, who lived in a village to the north near the Port of London, where the navy was based. Along with the civilian population of the island, two ladies – sisters, the Misses Burgess, I think they were called – from the

WVS (Women's Voluntary Service) would be put on board a ship and taken below deck to watch films during the tests. And, of course, there were the scientists and their staff from the AWRE (Atomic Weapons Research Establishment) at Aldermaston.

On November 8th, 1957, we at Main Camp were all lined up next to the road with our backs to the coconut trees and facing away from Ground Zero. All events would be relayed from the aircraft via Air Traffic Control and then via the loudspeakers. So, following all previous dummy run instructions, as the pilot reported, "The bomb has left the aircraft," we all sat facing away from the explosion with our hands pressed onto our closed eyes and our heads tucked into our knees. We were wearing just our tropical uniforms, but long trousers instead of shorts, and had no special safety equipment.

The tannoy began to count down the seconds before the bomb was due to explode. "Five ... four ... three ... two ... one ..." I could see the bones in my hands right there in front of my closed eyes; it was horrible, and I was very frightened. Then I could feel this immense heat travelling through my body. It was as if someone was holding an electric fire against my back and pushing it through me. I was that scared, against all orders I opened my eyes and looked. There was literally nothing but white. I could not even see the trees next to me. At that moment I thought I was dying or dead, but then I heard the tannoy counting up to 25, which was when we could turn around to look at the explosion.

When we did, it was so terrifying. A huge sun had appeared over the top of us, but it was fifty times larger than the real sun. For the first few moments you could not bear to look at it because it was like looking at the real sun on a hot day. At first it was a boiling, searing mass of bright light and then it glowed red and smoky, and clouds with lightning flashes in green were going across it. The thing was looming and growing above our heads. Knowing the nuclear bomb had been dropped only 20 miles from us made me feel really worried, and many others were too. Then an enormous stem appeared to be sucking the ocean up and a halo worked outwards from the bomb and evaporated all the clouds in its path. It was spreading outwards in all directions, toward us ...

Then there was an almighty crack and the island seemed to shudder as we were all hit by the shockwave, which actually bowled many over. Debris was scattered everywhere. The coconut trees were bending under the strain, and fronds hit us as they were blown with the hurricane blast.

When we went back to our tent it had caved in at one end, but it was only the guy ropes that had slackened and we soon put it right. However, the church roof wasn't so lucky. It had blown right off; it was a shame because the Gilbertese ladies from the village had plaited the coconut fronds and the roof had looked magnificent. There was extensive damage to a lot of the wooden structures too, and even some vehicles had been blown sideways although not damaged.

Dusty and I were detailed to go and wash a Canberra that had flown through the cloud collecting samples. We had to scrub the engine nacelles by hand, and the only protection we had was rubber gloves, wellingtons and a pair of denims. I was also given a crude face mask to replace a remote breathing apparatus I had started to use, but the straps were broken on the face mask so it was hard to breathe through. After about twenty minutes we were soaked to the skin as the highly radioactive water splashed back off the aircraft onto our clothing. Another two chaps took over whilst we underwent our decontamination, which, at the time, didn't sound much but knowing what I know now makes me think a lot about my health since that time 60 years ago. I was in and out of the shower and checked over by a man in a white suit and breathing apparatus. His radiation monitor was still clicking even after I'd been in the shower three times.

A week later I was being treated at sick quarters for lots of carbuncles on my neck and back, which I was told were tropical boils. The boils reoccurred for about half of my tour at Christmas Island and I still bear the scars to this day.

The following day there were a lot of dead fish on the tide line and, wearing gloves, we had to pick them up and place them in canvas bags. Later the gloves were also put in the bags so that told us that something wasn't right about it all.

Dusty and I, along with the rest of the guys, sometimes went snorkelling in the lagoon where there was a raft that some of us had made from oil drums and a few planks. I could not swim very far but could manage to dive down off the raft and swim back to it. One day I dived down and was looking at the colours of some of the marine life when suddenly everything went dark. At first, I thought I was blacking out, and I panicked. As I started back up to the raft, I realised the cause of the blackness was a giant manta ray. These are gentle, curious creatures but you do not want to be underneath one if it goes to rest on the bottom because they weigh about half a tonne. Normally, at the time, I was lucky if I could swim twenty yards, but that day I surpassed all my expectations by swimming – or dog paddling, or whatever – all the way back to shore. If ever my grandchildren get talking about swimming, this is always a talking point; they are quick to remind everyone how Granddad was taught to swim by a giant manta ray.

CHAPTER NINE

At Christmas it poured with rain and for a lot of the time some of us were employed digging trenches around the officers' tents and mess. It started raining in the morning and by the afternoon the water was up to our ankles. Most of the chaps who were off duty were out in it keeping cool. We usually shared all the goody bags that were sent to us for Christmas, and on Christmas Day we were served in our mess by the officers. The menu wasn't very different to our everyday meals, except for the pudding, which was traditional, albeit out of a tin.

A few days later we were bitten all over by bed bugs that had hatched in the seams of our tents, most probably initiated by the land crabs, which were usually run over by vehicles or killed by people who were frightened of them. Personally, I thought they were cute and in our tent we would feed them scraps from the mess; if they became a problem, we would chase them away. Bed bugs were a common occurrence in the tented accommodation and every couple of months one would have an infestation of the horrible things. We would leave everything except our washing equipment in situ and move to alternative accommodation for a couple of days while the sanitation squad let off a canister bomb of DDT in the tent and fastened it up. When we came back our tent and clothes reeked of DDT, but the bugs were gone. 'Captain Flit', so named because he flew an Auster aircraft each week spraying DDT over the camp, helped keep the flies and mosquitoes to a minimum.

Rumours usually spread very quickly around the camp and at the beginning of April 1958 there was talk of 'The Big One'. The loud speakers were testing every day, so we knew the rumours were true. Sure enough, the next day we began our dummy runs for the next test.

There were many stories going around, some of them quite alarming. One was that if the bomb fell too low it would cause a giant wave that would swamp the island, which was only five feet above sea level. Another story, which seemed very likely because it came from the boffins themselves and was quoted from a book by someone, was that if the bomb was lower in altitude it could break the coral island stem, which is made of living and dying coral that starts on the ocean floor and finally breaks surface and makes an island atoll after a few million years. This rumour was supported by the fact that a large fleet of DUKW land sea craft were utilised and would line the road beside us on the dummy runs. We would practise evacuating by all climbing aboard the vehicles on the command given by the voice over the tannoy.

April 28th, 1958, and we all lined up in our predetermined positions ready for the live run by the two Valiant bombers that were to carry out the test. We followed the same procedure as during the previous test, but this time some of us were wearing all-in-one anti-flash suits complete with hood and goggles that you could not see through. A message came over the tannoy that the Shackleton search aircraft that were patrolling around the area of the drop zone had radioed a Liberian tanker that was steaming at a steady eight knots in the general direction of the test. When it was explained to the captain of the tanker that he was heading straight into the drop zone of a hydrogen bomb, it was reported that the tanker about-turned and was doing an estimated twenty knots in the opposite direction. From the response of about 2000 men, the story lightened the tension a bit. However, the general atmosphere amongst the men was very quiet and, if they were like me, most were worried. "At least we will all go together if anything goes wrong," I thought. Some men were literally crying; it was horrible to hear. The chaplain was reading the Bible aloud and that was even more scary, as if he was expecting the worst to happen.

As with the last test, we all sat with our backs to Ground Zero and waited for the familiar countdown to begin. The last test yielded approximately 1.8 megatons. This one, Operation Grapple Y, would be much bigger at about 3 megatons, which we were told was equivalent to all the explosive force used in the Second World War. It would turn out to be Britain's only true hydrogen bomb and would put Great Britain into the superpower class.

The tannoy came to life and stated that the aircraft had reached Point Charlie and was live to drop on the countdown. The order came to close our eyes and wait for the second countdown once the device had exploded. But when the countdown reached zero, I felt nothing. Nor did I see anything like I did with Grapple X.

I panicked. Why was I not feeling or seeing what I expected? I lifted my goggles and, without even looking around, I was blinded momentarily by the extremity of the flash. For the next week I was seeing red balls in front of my eyes.

Even though I was half-blinded, when we were given the order to turn around and look at the bomb I saw an enormous fireball, much bigger than the last time, which was growing in width and height very quickly. It seemed to be coming for us, right over our heads. There were lots of colours moving in the cloud, and once again it was developing a spout under the huge dome; we'd been told that the spout was condensation being sucked up from the ocean and that it was a mile in diameter.

Just as before, the halo was working outwards from the bomb. When it reached us, it was as if the whole island had shaken in protest, and the crack and boom of the blast was louder and stronger than ever. Lots of us went head over heels as we were bowled over. Anything not fastened down was carried away and there was extensive damage all over the island. The tannoy came to life again and told us to board the DUKWs that were lined up, which we did. But before we had all got on them, the tannoy said, "Attention, all personnel may stand down." Apparently, they thought the wind had changed direction, but it was a false alarm.

I've often thought about that. What if the wind had carried the full radiation cloud onto Main Camp? In my opinion it would have been a disaster. To our east was the reef, south would have taken us nearer the bomb, and going west only led into the lagoon. That left the north, towards the Port of London, which was about seventeen miles away. In my opinion, we would never have got clear of the island in time.

Afterwards, I joined the queue for the doctor. Many of us

veterans of Grapple X were there with temporary blindness from looking too soon at Grapple Y; we should have been warned that we wouldn't feel the heat or see the shadow of our hands this time because of the protective equipment. The blindness lasted about a week and it was a miserable time for me. If I wanted to sleep, the red balls would change to blue when I closed my eyes, but when they were open it was like I had sand grit in them. The only relief I had was for about ten minutes after I applied eye drops.

That night it rained. The only clouds above the island were the remains of the bomb cloud. I didn't see it; my eyes were still too sore, so I stayed in the tent while the others ventured outside to cool down in the rain. Maybe that was my salvation. I am only speculating, but all these years later they are saying that the rain was 'black rain', contaminated with radiation from the cloud. So many of my fellow 'guinea pigs' have now passed on, many only in their fifties, and as I have not had any word for years about my friend Dusty, I wonder if he has passed too.

*An official photograph given to us after the successful test of the real
hydrogen bomb, Grapple Y, on the 28th April 1958.*

CHAPTER TEN

A couple of weeks later, Dusty and I went to a well-known location on the island where we could cast out fishing lines over the reef. But these were not ordinary fishing lines: they were nylon parachute cord, with a large hook and wire tracer attached. We were shark fishing.

We had been fishing for about two hours and all we seemed to catch were bone fish. They kept taking our bait, so we cut them up and put them on the hook for bait instead.

It was getting late in the afternoon. We were about to pack up and go back for our evening meal when all of a sudden I was literally dragged forward into the water. I had tied the parachute cord in a noose around my wrist whilst I read my book and the noose was cutting into my skin. I shouted out to Dusty as I was pulled in the shallows toward the reef. I could not get a footing on the slippery coral bottom and I was now being dragged toward the reef, face down. Dusty managed to grab my legs in time, enabling me to scramble to my feet, and between us we had a ten-minute fight to drag whatever it was on my hook onto the beach. Measured from nose to tail fin, it turned out to be a nine-foot shark. With the help of the army engineers and their winch truck we got the shark to the sergeants' mess. I should say, Dusty and the REME got it to the mess, because after being dragged along the coral I had to take my lacerated chest and legs to the hospital.

The medical officer kept me in overnight, after giving me a shot of antibiotics in my backside. He also painted my wounds with some kind of purple medication. The wounds were very painful, and the doctor said I would probably get coral poisoning, and I did.

I woke in the middle of the night to a commotion of groans and general movement of beds and equipment. Wondering if anything had gone wrong, I pressed the attendance buzzer. A male nurse came to speak with me, and I was informed that a group of Senior Non-Commissioned Officers (SNCOs) had been brought in from the sergeants' quarters after getting food poisoning from a meal they had eaten in their mess earlier that evening. He added: "I should keep quiet about the shark you sent to their mess if I were you, because that is what has given them this food poisoning." They were put in beds raised at the feet on books and had mostly recovered by mid-morning the next day after drinking milk and being sick all night long. I heard them say that if they found out who took the shark to the mess, they would drown him.

A few days went by and it was our turn to go on a week's leave back to Hawaii. Dusty and I took a Hastings to Hickham Field. We had been advised, unofficially, by a medical officer to get an Operation Grapple tattoo on our forearm, so that in the future if we went into a military hospital back in the UK the doctors would see the tattoo and take a blood count. I realise now after all these years what he was trying to tell us, without giving away any confidential medical information. However, since leaving the RAF I sent for my medical records and there is no mention of me having medical attention at Christmas Island. We got the tattoo, as advised.

On our return to Christmas Island, the two other chaps in our tent had gone and two new cooks were in their place. They were 'moonies' – RAF slang for someone without a sun tan – and by now we were very darkly sunburnt. I sent home a 'deep sea box' containing coconuts that were painted and varnished and had 'A Coconut from Christmas Island' painted on them, along with some clothes and other things that would lighten my load for flying back to the UK. Oh, and a shark tooth necklace made of some of the teeth from the shark we caught.

Before I forget, during my time at Christmas Island, we – the occupants of 222 Tent on Main Camp – had a pet crab. We named it Fred, but I haven't mentioned it until now because, to be honest, people think it was cruel to keep a wild creature in a hole next to our tent. But we always kept it well fed and gave it plenty of water, and as it was a land crab it did not need to go into the sea. At first, we kept it restrained, but after a short while we decided to let it go, but it always came back to the hole we had made it. It looked a lot like a giant hairy-legged spider.

Christmas Island land crab ... or giant hairy spider?

CHAPTER ELEVEN

In mid-October Dusty and I boarded an old Hastings that flew us to Fiji, which did not look much different to Christmas Island, except for the built-up areas of thatched dwellings that were scattered all over the island. Along with some men we had met on the aircraft, we bought postcards from a shop in the terminal building, but we could not leave the airport; we were only refuelling on our way to Darwin in Australia. The flight there seemed to take forever, but at last we landed. It was late afternoon and again we could not leave the airport, so we bedded down in the arrival building after getting a shower and some food.

The following day we set off for Singapore in the trusty old Hastings, which again wasn't the most comfortable aircraft I had flown in, but it was reliable.

Having landed at RAF Changi, which is about 20 miles from the city of Singapore, we were told that we were to be billeted at the RAF barracks for the next couple of days. The RAF station was very busy; it was quite large and also home to a big RAF hospital that aided all our services over there. We were told we would be flying in a Britannia to Bombay, India in two days so we had time to have a look around Singapore and perhaps do a bit of shopping. The lads on camp asked where we had come from because we were more tanned than them. When we told them about the hydrogen bombs, they thought it must have been exciting to see them let off that close. I reserved my feelings and comments on that, and so did Dusty.

A couple of the chaps in the billet asked us if we would like to go downtown with them. We jumped at the chance and we soon flagged a 'pick-up' taxi to take us to Singapore City. This is the cheapest method of getting from A to B and for 20 cents it would take you twenty miles or more, but what our guides lacked to mention was that the taxi would pick up and let off passengers anywhere along the route. By the time we reached our destination we had been sat on, squeezed and at one stage shared our ride with some chickens that were in a local resident's basket. Some of the time the Mercedes car, which normally carried five passengers, was filled with as many as eight people.

The two lads with us told us that in monsoon season the twenty-feet wide, deep concrete ditches (known as 'monsoon ditches') running alongside the roads would overflow with flood water and sometimes only large vehicles could travel on the roads. I noticed that a lot of the local women carried umbrellas made from palm leaf canopies on a bamboo frame and varnished with coconut oil, which was quite smelly, but today they were being used as sunshades as they walked along. In our Hawaiian shirts, shorts and flip flops we seemed to blend in with the population, because many people were dressed the same, except the Chinese, who wore their traditional black knee-length trousers and wide coned hats.

In the roadside markets (called 'armours markets') you could buy anything, but you had to haggle for it, and you had to be polite, and you had to answer to the name of 'John' if you were British or American! All we heard was, "You buy this, John," or "You buy that, John." Or, "This very good, John, you buy." Of course, most of the multi-nationals who lived there only knew a little English. We went to a bar and had a couple of lagers and then on for a meal at the Union Jack Club, which was near Raffles Quay and the famous Raffles Hotel. We were limited to what we could do in the time we were allotted before our flight, but we managed to get a few souvenirs. I liked Singapore and would have liked to have seen more of it.

Having boarded an RAF Britannia, it wasn't long before we left Singapore and were winging our way across an endless greenery of Malaysian jungle. The stewards on the aircraft were RAF and were male, and I remember feeling a little surprised as usually the air stewards were female. I must say, though, that the food served up for lunch on the aircraft was superb, much more palatable than that of the civilian airlines.

It came as a surprise to us when we were diverted to RAF Akrotiri in Cyprus, because there was bad weather happening in Bombay. As we approached Akrotiri it looked stunning in the late morning sunshine, with mountains looming on the skyline. We enjoyed a meal in the airmen's mess there, and again armed with pen and postcards from the NAAFI shop, we went into the NAAFI lounge and wrote our cards whilst having coffee and sandwiches.

All too soon we were winging our way over Europe and the Alps. We were getting very excited by now and could not wait to land back home in good old Blighty.

As we flew over the south coast and saw the white cliffs of

Dover or Dorset (I cannot remember which), everyone let out a massive cheer. Dusty and I had already exchanged addresses and promised to keep in contact; he lived in Wales and I was in Yorkshire. But after a few years we lost touch and, after getting no reply to several letters, I didn't pursue it. But it saddened me; we had had so many adventures together.

The journey by train from RAF Lyneham in Wiltshire seemed to take forever. It was three thirty in the afternoon when I arrived at Doncaster station, and I was overwhelmed by emotion when I saw my mum and sister Elsie waiting to meet me. We got a taxi home and I was overjoyed to be with my brothers and sisters again. Poor old Dad was still working in the fields and I ran off to see him. We had a very emotional reunion. I had never known my dad to cry but he did then, and so did I at seeing his pleasure turn to tears of emotion.

I had brought everyone a little something back and Mum fussed around me as if I had been away for years, although it did seem longer than a year. I remember that night at home as if it was yesterday: everyone asking what it was like going on an aircraft, and about the bomb, and all the different places I had seen. Dad made an awful smell by breaking in the new pipes I had brought him by burning the inside of the bowls with a red-hot poker.

My three weeks' disembarkation leave went much too quickly and my next posting was imminent. I had received my joining instructions to my next RAF station by post, which included rail warrants and instructions of travel, some of which would be by bus, for which I also had warrants. Before I left, I gave Mum an envelope and made her promise not to open it until the following day. In it, I had put three hundred pounds, which was some of the savings I had accrued during my overseas tour of duty.

CHAPTER TWELVE

I travelled by train from Doncaster to Birmingham New Street, via Sheffield and Derby. There I transferred to Birmingham Snow Hill to catch a train to Leamington Spa in Warwickshire. Finally, I took a bus to RAF Gaydon, which was about ten miles south of Leamington Spa on the A41.

I reported to headquarters and did all the necessary arrival procedure that I have already mentioned when one arrives at another station for a tour of duty. The station warrant officer was a very nice person and made me feel welcome. After a while he sat me down and had a good chat with me about what I wanted to do – meaning would I be interested in signing on for more years of service in order to get established in another trade? I replied that I would like to be a crash rescue fireman. He said he would get me sorted and within a couple of weeks I was a nine-year regular and on my way to RAF Catterick, the home of the Royal Air Force Regiment and the School of Fire Fighting.

During an eight-week course in Fire Crash and Rescue I learnt about Martin Baker ejection seats and how to make them safe before trying to get aircrew out of an aircraft, and how to fire off the canopy after making sure the ejection seat was safe. I also discovered that it was imperative that you knew how to make the armaments safe on all aircraft, in case they were armed. In the event that an aircraft's engines were still running, we learnt how to shut them down. We also had to know practically everything about firefighting, from the gallons per minute a pump could produce on each of the different fire vehicles down to tyre pressures. There was a lot to learn and it would not all be all learnt on the basic fire course; over the next twenty years I attended many more courses, and many practice hot fires, where we had to put out aircraft fires whilst carrying out a rescue on a dummy mannequin constructed from a pair of denims filled with sand to the average weight of a grown man. We were also taught how to carry out first aid and resuscitation. The advanced first aid training came later; one took the advanced course at RAF Hospital Halton, near High Wycombe in Buckinghamshire. There were many courses at different locations, which I will mention at length in later chapters.

I went back to RAF Gaydon as a trained fireman, but after only two months I was off again, back to Catterick to do driving training. I spent two weeks training on 4x4s, then two more weeks on six-wheelers, followed by another fortnight on eight-wheelers before I took the road test and several operational tests, where you were tested on an actual hot fire practice ground. And there were many more driving courses to come.

When I got back to RAF Gaydon, I met Derek – who went on to become my brother-in-law. My billet was located next to the domestic fire station in the main camp, and Derek had the bed space next to mine. Our place of duty was the airfield at the crash bays next to the air traffic control centre but during flying, those of us on duty would be located permanently at the crash bays and all the other crews would be sent off duty. In the event of a fire anywhere on the base, we would only go to it if there was no imminent danger to aircraft, including those landing, in circuit, or taking off, and only then at the discretion of the duty air traffic controller. If there were any circumstances where an aircraft needed immediate fire coverage, domestic fires on the base would have to be dealt with by the normal civilian fire brigade.

During the Cold War, Victor and Valiant Bombers were based at Gaydon RAF Station, in constant readiness for an imminent strike on a potential enemy. They were armed with a nuclear deterrent, which at that time was the Blue Steel Missile, and it had to have specialist crash cover. We were on constant alert and, like the aircrews manning the bombers, we were on a four-minute warning scenario.

The propellant of the Blue Steel Missiles was hydrogen peroxide, which could become very unstable if a catalyst was introduced, so our crash crews needed yet more specialist training to deal with this.

In 1961, I met a local girl. Her name was Christine; she had a twin sister, Anne, and they lived in the village of Knightcote, about five miles from RAF Gaydon. Christine and her mother worked as cleaners in the sergeants' mess and they walked past the domestic fire section each night to get to the guardroom to clock off work. This was how I met her, and I then introduced her sister Anne to my crew mate Derek.

Derek and Anne, and Christine and I were married in a double wedding ceremony at Burton Dassett church on 27th October 1961.

Initially, we all moved in to Christine and Anne's parents' house in Knightcote. However, my wife and I eventually moved into a caravan on RAF Gaydon's official caravan park. On 28th March 1962, our daughter Angela was born. Shortly after her birth she developed tuberculosis, but fortunately, after five or six years of medication, she was cured.

Later that year we were on duty one October night when we heard a loud metallic bang, and fire bells sounded to alert us that an emergency may be pending. We listened on the radio as a message came over instructing us to proceed to the western crash gate. This was one of several specially weakened gates situated all around the airfield to allow our crash vehicles access by smashing through them without having to stop.

We then received confirmation that Victor Bomber XA934 had crashed in a wood just beyond the village of Combrooke, only a few miles beyond the runway where it had just taken off. The noise we heard was a malfunction in an engine, which severed the fuel lines to the other engines. The pilot very bravely managed to avoid the village but sadly there was only one survivor, the co-pilot, who ejected safely. We finally got to the crash site but were hampered by not being able to get near enough quickly enough because of the dense woodland.

In February 1965 the Valiant Bombers were disbanded after cracks were found in the wing spars. That just left the Victors at RAF Gaydon.

CHAPTER THIRTEEN

Christine was five months pregnant with our second child when I received news that I was to be posted to Singapore. My application to extend my regular service to 22 years had also been approved. This meant I would receive a much better wage.

Before I went abroad I had to take an advanced fire course, which was required before one could be promoted, so off I went to Catterick again for five weeks. I passed the course, was promoted to corporal and received a posting to RAF Tengah in Singapore following embarkation leave. However, there was one drawback. Christine would not be able to fly out there with me until I had found us accommodation. Unfortunately, that was the rule, and I didn't like the idea of her having to travel without me all that way, in her pregnant state and with a four-year-old child to look after as well. Plus she'd never even been on a train before, never mind a nine-thousand mile trip on an aircraft.

It was a worrying time, especially because women were not allowed to fly in pressurised aircraft after seven and a half months of pregnancy, so time was short.

I flew from Heathrow on a Britannia via Istanbul in Turkey, which was only a refuelling stop. Then we went on to

Bombay. When they opened the cabin door we were hit by a tremendous heat; it was midnight local time and really hot. I managed to buy some postcards and sent them off in the little time we had at the airport.

We were soon taking off again, this time to fly the rest of the way nonstop. I spent the first fifteen minutes watching blue flames coming out of the exhausts and that's all I remember until an air hostess woke me by shaking my shoulder. "Fasten your seat belt, sir. We are about to land."

We landed at Singapore International Airport in the afternoon. It seemed a lot cooler than the last time I was there. After a long wait to get my cases off the moving belt I walked through customs and saw an airman in khaki drill uniform standing near the exit, holding a board that simply said, 'RAF Tengah'. I approached him. "Are you posted to Tengah?" he asked. I nodded. He pointed to a white service bus and told me to put my luggage in the open boot.

The ride to RAF Tengah was a real eye opener. The driving skills of some of the locals was nothing less than stupid and I actually lost count of the number of accidents that held us up on the main Bukit-Timor highway. But it was something we would have to get used to.

I arrived at RAF Tengah and got organised at headquarters and fitted out in the fire section billet. Then I went on to the crash bays, where I met the regiment officer in charge and the warrant officer, who was the equivalent of manager/SNCO in charge of the fire section. There I was given my place on B Crew and told what my position was – I was in fact to be the new JNCO in charge of B Crew, to whom I was about to be introduced. There were sixteen men in each crew, including one sergeant, two corporals, five drivers/firemen, and eight firemen, who were allocated positions on each of the tenders.

On the base were two squadrons of Javelin aircraft belonging to 60 Squadron and 64 Squadron. There was also 20 Squadron, who had Hunters, and the Canberras of 45 Squadron. There were always other aircraft visiting, including Buccaneers, Victor Bombers, English Electric Lightnings and Gannets. It was the busiest airfield I was ever stationed at in my capacity as a fire, crash and rescue fireman. When I arrived at Tengah in 1965 there were around 30 Javelin aircraft between the two squadrons but when I left three years later there were only nine left, which had been amalgamated into just one squadron, 64 Squadron.

Christine and my little daughter Angela finally arrived a month later, after I had rented a bungalow across the straights in Johore. It was actually in Malaysia, but as it was only twenty miles from Tengah it was a temporary solution until I got a married quarter in Singapore.

Living in the bungalow next door to us was a land-based Royal Navy sailor and his wife, who were very friendly towards us. They proved to be friends indeed because when my wife went into the British Military Hospital at Bukit Timor to have our son John, who was five weeks premature, our neighbours took care of Angela for us. John was born a 'blue baby' and had to have a series of blood procedures in which we almost lost him.

By the time he came out of hospital, we had already moved into a married quarter at Pacific Mansions on River Valley Road in the centre of Singapore City. We were on the fourteenth floor of a block of flats eighteen storeys high, which had been allocated to the British Forces families by the

Singapore authorities.

It was luxury! Three bedrooms, a lounge and a separate kitchen and dining room, all with tiled flooring except for the lounge, which had carpet. The three bedrooms had their own adjoining bathrooms and toilets, and my wife employed a maid to do the housework for a small sum of money compared to my wages. I even received RAF transport to the camp. The only downside was the inconvenience of using the lifts every time you went out, and on the odd occasion we had to walk up and down all the stairs when the lifts were out of order.

These skyscraper flats were being built in abundant numbers and it always puzzled me how they got away with their building regulations. They always used bamboo scaffolding and women carried cement on their heads up the ladders connecting the different storeys of the new building. I also noticed part of a cement bag stuck in the concrete of our flat's balcony.

The monsoon season had started by then and it rained continually for three months from January to the end of March. The rain came down without a break, much like a continuous thunderstorm, and now I understood why there were twenty feet wide by twenty feet deep concrete ditches on each side of the roads, which channelled into larger and larger ditches until the water emerged into the China Sea. Even then, most of the time, only the larger vehicles such as buses and lorries were able to wade through the water as the ditches overflowed.

One evening, while on duty, I had taken over command of the crew whilst the sergeant in charge went for his evening meal at the sergeants' mess. The crash alarm sounded, and the radio informed us that a 20 Squadron Hawker Hunter was coming in to land with problems. I directed the crash crew vehicles to the intersection of the main runway. During that era, goose neck flares were used as emergency runway lighting and it was our task to go down the runway and light them. On this particular occasion the flares had already been lit because the runway lighting was off. (If you're not familiar with these types of flare, they are basically a garden watering can filled with kerosene, with a wick protruding from the spout that was lit at night.)

The aircraft landed with one wheel on the runway and one on the grass. The wing tanks of the Hunter were slung under the wings, and the tank on the side where the wheel had sunk into the grass ruptured, leaving a stream of fuel behind the aircraft, which in turn was ignited by the flares.

I directed one foam tender to make a blanket of foam between the fire and the aircraft where it had come to rest. Meanwhile, I directed another foam vehicle to lay a blanket of foam around the Hunter, noting that there was no fire around the aircraft. All the goose necks flares were extinguished with a water spray.

My number two and I approached the Hunter on an aircraft rescue truck. It carried one hundred and fifty pounds of a dry powder fire extinguishing agent, which wasn't needed in this case. My number two went to the cockpit to make the seat safe but it was empty. The pilot was standing fifty yards away, having cut the engines. I noticed that the Hunter was still armed with live rockets under the wing, so I went underneath the wing, which was positioned over the grass, to apply the weapons safety break. This entailed undoing a bayonet coupling that was located in a quick release hatch under the wing. The wheel had sunk into the soft earth and not much of the wheel strut was left showing above the ground. I had just completed making the weapons safe when I felt myself being pulled by my legs until I was clear of the wing. I had been very lucky – the wing was slowly sinking down to ground level and the wheel and strut were soon completely submerged in the mud. It was a unique demonstration of how a crash crew must work together as a team and look out for each other.

After we had everything under control an ambulance and doctor arrived along with a tug master to get the aircraft out of the hole. However, it was decided by a technician that a crane would be required to lift the aircraft and get PSP plating under the wheel.

The commanding officer commended us for our professionalism, and a few months later, the SNCO in charge of the crash crew (who wasn't actually present that night) was awarded a British Empire Medal for the incident. This is something that happens very often in the forces.

CHAPTER FOURTEEN

A few weeks later, just after the monsoon was over, we were out in front of the crash bays, servicing equipment on the fire tenders, when we heard some ducks quacking. They were at the bottom of the monsoon ditch, which was now empty of water but very muddy. One of the ducks was so caked in mud it couldn't fly and a couple of us managed to catch it.

After killing the bird, we washed it clean and, as the mud washed away, it became obvious it was a white duck. We had just taken it to the rest room and put it in our oven when four officer aircrew walked in demanding an explanation for why we had stolen one of their mascot ducks. Someone from the building next to ours had witnessed us capturing the duck and informed 20 Squadron that "the crash crew have just killed one of your mascots." Of course, we began to deny it – until one of the aircrew produced white feathers from our dustbin. All we could do was explain that because of the mud we initially thought it was a wild duck. The other corporal on our crew, an Irishman who was always full of 'blarney', made the situation worse by asking them if they would like to stay to dinner.

The RAF station produced a weekly paper and the following week the headline of *The Tengah Times* read:

'Crash Crew Cannibals Eat Twenty Squadron Mascot'.

The Gloucester Javelins of 60 and 64 Squadron were dwindling fast. Some crashed into the sea, some crashed too far away in the jungle for us to get to, while others were pirated for parts for other aircraft. We were always busy attending incidents with them. So it was decided by the powers that be that some of us would have to complete courses on jungle and sea survival at RAF Seletar, which was also in Singapore. This would be an aircrew course and was to be completed by myself and eight other NCOs from Tengah, Seletar and Changi stations.

After reporting to the parachute and survival section at RAF Seletar, we spent a week in the classroom, where the instructors taught us what to eat and what not to eat. This included snakes, grubs and other naturally available foods – like the edible inner bark of a certain type of tree, which looks a bit like celery. We also learned how to make a beach oven: you dug a hole, lined it with large stones, then lit a fire in it. When it had been lit for an hour you raked out the ashes, wrapped your snake or whatever in large leaves and buried it. Two hours later you dug it up and your food was cooked. We were taught how to use a compass and an aircrew map, which are the only maps that a crashed aircrew would have in the event of bailing out. In fact, the only equipment we were to carry with us was what the crashed aircrew would have: a map, a compass, a parachute, a first aid pack, a 9mm revolver and a clip of ammunition, and a survival knife. We were also shown how to catch snakes, poisonous or otherwise, and prepare them to eat. If you cut the snake's head off two inches back from its eyes, this gets rid of the poison glands. Once you've removed its inedible parts, which we learned to identify, it is then ready to cook. It tastes like chicken.

Fern leaf tops are the little curly leaves at the top of the plant. When wrapped in a piece of parachute material and dipped in boiling water, these make a nice cup of 'fern leaf tea'. We were also taught how to make our camp shelter from branches and small trees and how to utilise our parachutes as hammocks strung between the trees – all while in enemy-occupied territory.

After the lessons, we had specialist training on mounting and dismounting a helicopter by rope whilst it hovered over the place of 'rope up' or 'rope down'.

All that completed, we were conveyed by helicopter to a remote part of the Malaysian jungle up near Kota Tinggi. We were flown up the eastern coast of Malaysia, then dropped off in a predetermined place about fifty miles from anywhere in dense jungle. When we arrived, we roped down into one of the few rare clearings. We had to survive for three weeks whilst negotiating the jungle terrain in order to travel to another clearing twelve miles north east. One may think that twelve miles in three weeks should be 'a piece of cake', but until one has travelled in primary and secondary mixed jungle, one should think again.

Water, or lack of it, is one consideration for delaying travel in the Malaysian jungle. Some areas have abundant rivers and streams whereas others have none. You can supplement your water supplies by collecting water from pitcher plants and straining the many insects out of it using filters made from parachute material. In any case, the medical pack included water purification tablets that you used if you didn't or couldn't boil the water. Although it may look dirty it would be safe to drink. We also had iodine; this was not just for treating wounds but was used extensively for making leeches come out from where they had burrowed their heads under your skin and bloated themselves on your blood. If you pulled them away with your fingers, you ran the risk of leaving their teeth under your skin, which would need surgery to remove. There were many de-leeching stops during our trek through the jungle.

To move efficiently through the jungle, you had to work as a team. There were ten of us (including the instructor) and we moved in single line, one behind the other. At the front was the machete man, who chopped any obstacle that got in our way. Next was the compass man, then the map man, and after him came the pace man. Every four steps represented a yard and every fifty yards he would make a notch on a stick; he and the chap behind him would count every step and confirm with each other. The sixth man collected water from pitcher plants as he walked, in case our supplies got short further along the trek. Numbers seven, eight and nine would catch any snakes that might be pointed out by the others, avoiding the venomous ones for obvious reasons. Number ten was the instructor and he took up the rear guard. He also took up the rear position because if anyone stopped, they could become hopelessly lost within minutes if they lost touch with the others.

The instructor stopped us at 16.00 hours and told us to make camp. We made up three three-man shelters in case it rained. Some of us looked for dry sticks to make a fire; others cut up three snakes, as instructed, and we made a beach oven to cook them in.

We had collected water from a stream on the way, so the pitcher plant water was kept for an emergency. I noticed the instructor empty a sachet into his tin mug of hot water and I asked him what the sachet contained. He just tapped the side of his nose as if to say, "Keep this out." I found out later that he had a supply of Maggi soups. And to be quite honest, if I had to keep training people in jungle survival, I would too.

The snakes were put into the beach oven and covered up. I made a cup of the fern leaf tea, which was quite revolting, so I just drank water instead. At least we all had to try it. I found one of the celery-like trees and cut it open and tried it … well, to say it was like celery was stretching the truth, but it wasn't bad at all. Once the snakes were cooked, they looked horrible. They were skinned like a banana and chopped into sections like salmon steaks. My first taste was taken reluctantly, but it was quite nice, so I had seconds after everyone had got their piece. Anyway, I think it went down well because there wasn't any left.

I made my parachute hammock, stringing it between two trees, and tied my poncho ground sheet above it. Being canvas, it would stop me getting wet through if it rained. However, I was woken very early in the morning by a horrible giant insect crawling over me; in my semi-conscious state, it was the smell that I noticed first. I shouted, because some of the others called out to ask if I was alright. How did I explain that a ten-inch long millipede was crawling over me while I was four feet off the ground without someone asking if I had been dreaming? I think it came down the tree and along my hammock. But it disappeared before anyone else saw it, so every now and then I heard remarks like, "Seen any more giant millipedes lately, Coggy?" (My surname being Coggon, this was my nickname.)

We had covered three miles on our first week in the

jungle; the instructor was pleased, because other teams on their first week had usually only completed two miles. We had to check our boots in the mornings to make certain there were no giant black scorpions in them. Although this species was the biggest in Malaysia, they were not the most poisonous. The very small brown ones from the Sahara Desert were the most lethal of all the scorpion family. Tree spiders are also large but not venomous; however, they can give a person a nasty bite, and giant centipedes can too. It is a fact that most insects are large in the jungle, but on the plus side, virgin jungle is sterile so no matter how wet you got you would not catch a common cold – unless one of your party took it in when they started the course.

During the second week we came to a river that wasn't fast flowing, but to be on the safe side we all lashed together with parachute cord. The deepest part of the river came up to my chest and it took my breath away, as it was ice cold.

The last week was hard going. We were hungry and it made us eat things we would never normally touch. I reckon I must have lost a stone in weight. We were also getting welts all over our bodies from leeches. They were nasty little creatures and we had to bear their persistent gnawing while we were moving, because to stop every time we felt them would mean stopping every five minutes. When we did stop, we had to help each other get the critters off our bodies.

By the last week we had all taken turns in the team to do every job: navigating using the map, snake catching etc. Finally, we came to the arranged clearing marked on our map; we had, at last, finished the first part of the course.

That afternoon the helicopter arrived to pick us up. The winch man threw down the rope ladder, which you must never touch until it earths with the ground or you could get a very nasty static electric shock. We all 'roped up' and set off back to RAF Seletar.

The next stage was the sea survival course and after two days in the classroom we were taken out in a Zodiac rubber rescue launch powered by a large Evenrude outboard engine. Rubber dinghies were dropped over the side, followed by us in full aircrew kit – including Mae Wests, an anti-G suit and flying boots, again replicating aircrew who have ditched into the sea.

The launch that dropped us over the side kept going around us, making large waves whilst we struggled to swim to the dinghies. When at last we got to a dinghy we then had to fasten four solar stills (distillation balloons) on a long string and blow them up once we had poured sea water into them. Each balloon had a small charcoal filter on the bottom and an inner balloon inside the large outer one. The balloons were towed along behind the dinghy in the sea and, as the heat from the sun started the sea water evaporating, the condensed water began to collect in the larger balloon, then into the filter, and finally into a container as desalinated drinking water. This procedure went on for four hours until we had collected the four small amounts of desalinated water we needed to drink.

That completed the second part of our course. The next part involved us being trained as coxswains for the rubber Zodiac rescue craft. First, we were taught how to put the craft together – inflating it, putting the backboard and spine in the hull and fitting the outboard motor – and maintain it. Then, out on the water, we learnt what to do and what not to do, which was mainly common sense. Like, should you be travelling at a high speed then the craft must be slowed down to a stop gradually, otherwise the back wash will catch you up and swamp the craft over the stern.

That day we were allowed home with our new certificates of achievement. Christine and my children did a double take at my appearance: I'd grown a five-week beard and was two stone lighter.

CHAPTER FIFTEEN

Sometime later in the year we had a call out to a Canberra on the dispersal; an electrical fire had occurred in the cockpit. I managed to get into the cockpit and release the pilot, who was conscious but had been overcome by smoke whilst trying to exit the aircraft.

We were also called to quite a few barrier engagements, one being an English Electric Lightning that had missed the RHAG (Rotary Hydro Arrester Gear), which was there to slow the aircraft down quickly. We helped the two aircrew out of the Lightning, which had the crash barrier netting wrapped around it, disabling their exit.

The RHAG system consisted of two large barrels, each about ten feet in diameter, which were sunk into the ground, one directly opposite the other on either side of the runway. Built into the barrels were large paddles that were attached to a central shaft that extended out of the top of the tanks onto a pulley. Attached to the pulley was a drum of cable that stretched across the runway. Threaded on the cable were twenty thick hard rubber discs, about twelve inches in diameter, that kept the cable at a constant height of six inches above the runway surface. These discs were spaced out so as not to interfere with the central part of the runway where other aircraft may use it. The tanks were filled to a certain capacity with water. When an aircraft hook caught the cable, the pulley was turned, enabling the paddles to rotate while being restrained by the water, thereby slowing down the aircraft.

As the fire crew, we had the task of spacing out the rubber discs and servicing the RHAG with water, all under supervision of the duty engineer. We also needed to remove the wire from the runway or put it back, as requested by air traffic control.

During my second year of duty at RAF Tengah I went on detachments to Borneo and Malacca, but the one I want to relate to you concerns my trip to Kuantan in the state of Pahang.

I was given the task of taking a Mk Va fire tender, which is a large foam tender, from RAF Changi in Singapore to RAF Kauntan in Malaysia, a distance of 231 miles on jungle roads. I was to take with me one of our seconded local firemen, who was Malaysian and could act as an interpreter if it was necessary. Amad was a good fireman but he wasn't a driver and I asked if it was possible to supply a relief driver – to which the answer was no, they did not have a spare driver, and they would be pushed anyway while I was away.

The journey took us over the straights of Johore Baharu on almost deserted roads through Tebrau and Ulutiram, where we stopped in a layby on a deserted section of the road to take a cool shower from the water pump using the spray nozzle of the hose reel. Once we'd left the Bukit Timor dual carriageway in Singapore, we had only seen the odd timber lorry all morning. We were both completely naked showering beside the road when three tourist buses came past us with lots of beeping hooters and cheers and shouts! We could only stand there with our bare backsides to the road until the coaches had gone.

We stopped the night at a hotel in Kota Tinggi that had been recommended by the officer in charge of the mechanical transport section at RAF Changi. On Amad's advice we ate a meal of rice and something at the hotel – which, to be honest, wasn't the type of hotel I had expected. It was just a wooden building with a coconut frond roof, more like a typical Malay family dwelling in a typical kampong (village), and we were to sleep on mats on the floor.

Early the following morning Amad recommended another meal, consisting once again mainly of rice with fish. We set off after doing a physical check of the vehicle's equipment and fuel.

We went over a mountain road that was very narrow and quite scary; we could see the treetops far below. According to our map this was Bukit Samsu, which was near Ula Sungai where we planned to stop for a late lunch. I parked the truck in the yard next to a building that Amad chose for us to have another meal, which proved to be the best food so far. Local time being 1400 hours, I decided to press on to Ladang Sungai Ambat, where we would spend the night. It was proving to be slow going because the dangerous roads were often very narrow; sometimes they were flooded and had to be forded. We eventually parked up for the night and I told Amad that after our meal I would prefer to sleep in the fire vehicle, on the long seat provided for crew whilst travelling to an incident.

The following day we made better progress and by midday we had reached the ferry at Kampung Mengkasar. It looked perilous: the ferry didn't look big enough to get us over the wide river. However, I felt better when Amad told me that logging vehicles and tourist coaches used it. Anyway, it was the route given to me by Form 658, my authorisation for driving the vehicle.

The ferryman spoke in Malaysian to Amad, who translated what he said. He wanted to know the weight of the tender. I told him, via Amad, that I could empty the seven hundred gallons of water if need be. And that was what I did. This being satisfactory, we then crossed the river without any problem. But later there was a river at Kuantan that also needed to be crossed by ferry, so, as it was getting dark, we booked in at a hotel before we drove the last part of our journey.

The following morning, we passed over the river and delivered the fire truck to the MT section at RAF Kuantan. During the handover it was brought to my attention that the vehicle's suction hose had been stolen at our last stop, because it was certainly on the vehicle the morning before. The MT officer in charge wrote it off as stolen and informed the Malaysian police. It wasn't our fault.

We were flown back to Seletar in a Sunderland flying boat. It was a fantastic flight and we skimmed over the jungle treetops, sometimes low enough to see the leaves on the trees plainly. We were also invited to sit in the cockpit for a while, until it was time to land in the sea near RAF Seletar.

Alongside my military activities, I attended art classes at Singapore University where I attained an A Level. Later, some of my paintings were sold and reproduced without my permission at the many roadside and indoor markets in Singapore. However, this was a common fraud and was happening on a wide scale all over the Far East. I also studied basic electronics as a correspondence course, which I eventually passed. This put me in a good position for a course I would take later, during my career in radio and television servicing.

During my stay in Singapore I enjoyed the way of life that would help me understand multicultural communities and their ways and religions. Everyone worked together in harmony and this is an outlook that I have always found natural.

I have worked with almost every nationality and colour and we never showed any partiality to each other. It seems today that comments on social media and in the press can be misinterpreted by some people as abuse, but in the forces we got on with everyone, wherever they were from.

My two and a half years in Singapore would be up in two months' time but before then I was detached to Borneo for three weeks. Then it was time to pack our sea crates ready for their journey home to England, which I was getting impatient to see again.

If I could choose anywhere else in the world to live, it would be either Malaysia or Singapore. A particular favourite of mine was Malacca in Malaysia, where I served one of my many detachments providing fire cover for a practice bombing range.

CHAPTER SIXTEEN

I received news that my brother had contracted a fatal rat disease after trapping his thumb in a farm bailing machine and was in a coma in Doncaster Royal Infirmary. My family and I were given priority seats on a RAF VC 10 transport aircraft. We landed at Brize Norton and made our way to my wife's parents, who put up Christine and our children while I dashed back to Doncaster.

I was too late. My brother had passed away that morning. According to the doctor, Jim had Weil's disease, which had only been diagnosed twice at Doncaster Royal Infirmary, and both patients – one of them being my brother – had died.

My parents and siblings were of course devastated by Jim's death, but his wife was the worst affected. Janet was heavily pregnant with their first child – a child who would never meet their daddy. The heartbreak was terrible for everyone.

Jim had worked on the farm where my dad had become foreman. One night, Jim had come home with his thumb bandaged up. He went to the local doctor who, after cleaning and bandaging the wound, sent him home. This was on the Friday night. The next day he felt ill but was a bit better later, so he went to the local pub with my father for a couple of pints. However, on the way home (a two-mile walk) he felt poorly again. The next day he kept falling asleep and, in the end, he could not stand the pain his body was going through. He was sent to the infirmary where, after having his thumb seen to, it was found to be broken as well as cut. He was also diagnosed with Weil's disease. He was given sedative injections for the pain but died a while later, when his heart gave out because of the strong drugs.

After the funeral I went back to my family in Warwickshire for my disembarkation leave. Then I was posted to Brize Norton. Within a week we moved into a married quarter at Witney, not far from the base. My daughter Joanne was born there later.

Not a great deal happened at Brize Norton on the fire section; it was pretty quiet except for detachments to Germany and Cyprus. I also took part in many exercises that would take me to Libya and all over the British Isles.

One of these exercises was to an island off the coast of Scotland, RAF Stornoway. This place was a wild, windswept area, but I found it had a lot of attractions, such as the sea bird colonies that lived on the island in large numbers. What did surprise me, though, was the local people's way of life. Shops did not open on Sundays; it was much like an older version of England during the war years.

RAF Troodos in Cyprus was another interesting place. The weather during my short detachment was much the same as at home in England, but the base was in the mountains of Cyprus, so that is where the comparison ended.

Meanwhile, back at Brize Norton, the building of the largest hangar in the United Kingdom was completed. I saw the hangar, which was about the size of three football pitches of floor space. The first occupant was the Short Belfast transport aircraft, which was far too big to fit in the conventional hangars at most airfields. Later, VC10s were serviced in there too.

During my time at Brize, I took on a part time job at Globe Taxis in Witney, where we lived. I also worked part time for a coach company in Bampton. Unofficially, this was tolerated by the RAF because times were hard for some forces families and the wages were not very high.

However, I do recall getting an ear wagging from the station warrant officer … The fact was that I was one of three firemen at Brize driving the same bus part time, so we would park the bus on the drill square for each other to pick up the following morning. He fell out with us for that!

After three years at Brize I received an unaccompanied posting to the Middle East, to RAF Masirah in the Gulf of Oman. I had to move my family into unaccompanied married quarters at RAF Wellsbourne Mountford, near Stratford upon Avon.

CHAPTER SEVENTEEN

RAF Masirah was a desert island in the Sultanate of Oman and this place, away from my family, was to be my home for one year. The island was a barren piece of desert with no appeal to anyone who went there, in my opinion.

When on duty at the crash bays there was rarely any air movement that required our services, so we would move the vehicles out of the crash bay garage and play badminton all day – we even had the court marked out on the garage floor – or we would play volleyball outside, or five-a-side football in the many courts on the RAF camp. We even played inter league away matches when there were no air movements scheduled.

When there were movements, we had to remain in our silver asbestos suits for the duration, and very often, when everyone else on the camp was stood down to their air-conditioned billets, we had to sweat in our suits with temperatures sometimes in the nineties or hundreds.

One of the wonders of the world happens right here on this island, and it happens almost to the hour on a given night of the year, every year, depending on the moon phase. Giant turtles lay their eggs on the shore in the sand dunes; some of them travel thousands of miles across the ocean to get here on this particular night to lay their eggs at the same time as hundreds of other turtles. It is a very strange phenomenon. How do they even find their way back each year? Most of them have come every year of their adult life. It is a very laborious task. I have watched them struggle up the beach, some flipping their way through the sand up to a quarter of a mile from the sea, then scraping a hole about one cubic metre deep into the sand and depositing approximately 200 eggs into the hole. By the time she has finished burying her eggs in the sand, she is exhausted and usually takes frequent rests on her way back to the sea.

The Bedouin Arabs usually come the following morning and dig the eggs up. They take half of them and leave the rest to hatch, thereby ensuring – to their minds – that the cycle will keep going. But alas, when the baby turtles hatch, they have to dash to the sea and the remainder of the hatch is halved again by hungry seagulls. And then, after reaching the sea, other predators further reduce their number again by half, leaving probably fifty out of two hundred baby turtles that actually reach adulthood.

Some of the Bedouins have a strangely cruel but effective way of ensuring the baby turtles reach the water safely. They bait a fishing hook and catch a seagull. Then they remove the bird's flight feathers and tie it to a post. The screaming bird wards off the other seagulls from the area. However, there is only one winner here: the cruel Arab who steals fifty per cent of the eggs in the first place.

If we were off duty, we would go on desert treks around the island, climbing small mountains and exploring wadis, and sometimes getting stuck. We also did desert survival training.

Eventually I ran out of constructive things to do so I planted a garden with banana trees. By watering them every day I got a few bananas to grow, but donkeys, camels or humans must have stolen them because they never lasted long enough to go yellow. Talking of donkeys, the local Arabs were, in my opinion, very cruel to their animals. They loaded them up until the poor little creatures staggered under the weight and they would keep hitting them with their sticks to make them walk until they dropped; they even hit them whilst they were down. When the donkeys were hobbled, they were given cardboard boxes to eat. I make no excuse for not liking Bedouin Arabs for this very reason. Perhaps it's because I love animals more than most people; I don't rightly know.

One day, while we were on duty, I was on the rescue truck when air traffic control directed us to go in Crash One (the ACRT Land Rover) to scare a donkey away from the approach of the runway in use. When we arrived, the donkey was situated right on the very edge of the touchdown area, and even driving around the donkey only made it shift a few yards towards the end of the runway. It was then that we noticed the aircraft approaching was a Vulcan bomber. My number two radioed the tower and I drove off the approach and fired a red Verey pistol to warn the aircraft of danger on the runway. As the aircraft pulled up into a steep climb, the poor donkey was blown like a spinning top onto rocks on the undershoot. When we found him, the poor little animal was dead and badly mutilated. The owner wanted compensation, I heard, but he was refused because there was a tribal ruling made by the sultan that their animals were to be kept clear of aircraft movements.

Sometimes life in Oman was very boring so I took it upon myself to paint our restroom with a mural, so it would be like looking out of a log cabin's windows. I painted the walls like jointed logs stacked one on top of another in authentic colours of old wood. Then I added two large windows looking out into a meadow with horses in it and mountains in the background. It took me almost my last six months to complete, but I did finish it, and everyone liked the end product. Even the commanding officer commented about it approvingly on his inspection. However, I cannot claim full credit for the mural because someone before me had originally started it; I just added a lot to it.

Soon it was time to go home, but the unaccompanied tour had played havoc with my family life. Because that part of my story is my own private business I will not be saying much about it, but what I can say is that I do not blame anyone; I can only blame forces life in general. It can be a wonderful life for a single person, but for married couples it is not good. But this, of course, is my opinion and should not reflect anyone else's thoughts on the matter.

Oil painting of Vulcan XH 558, G F Coggon, 2012

CHAPTER EIGHTEEN

My next posting was to RAF Scampton in Lincolnshire. My family moved into a married quarter straight away and my children went to school at the base. For the first three months everything was working out fine. But then a ghost from my days away on my unaccompanied tour at Masirah decided to follow us to Scampton. The incident was settled amicably, and our family stayed united for the children's sake. Thank goodness the problem has stayed away since.

I liked RAF Scampton. It was home to V bombers, which consisted of Vulcans and Victors. The Vulcans kept us busy because they needed a 'hot wheel' check every time they landed, which was very often, with three squadrons flying most days.

These checks were carried out by my number two and me, plus two other crew members. Driving out on the ACRT, with chocks carried on the back, we would wait near the end of the runway, then contact the pilot by radio through air traffic control. Then, with the pilot's acknowledgement, I would go under the aircraft's nose and plug in my throat mike to wait for a break in the inter cockpit radio transmissions whilst they completed after-flight checks. I would call the pilot and ask if the crash crew could chock the wheels for a fire check. He would respond by saying we were clear to chock the wheels. Then I would signal to my two men to chock the aircraft. When it was chocked, I would tell the pilot we had the wheels chocked and ask him to release the brakes. My chaps would go around the 'boogies' – the aircraft landing gear – checking for hot wheel brake drums and for any possible venting of fuel onto the wheels. After the check I would say to the pilot, "You are clear to taxi, please apply brakes," and he would say, "Brakes on." That would be the sign for me to give a hand signal to my two crewmen to clear the chocks away from under the aircraft. My last message to the pilot would be: "Chocks clear – you will be clear to taxi on my signal from the port side," (which is, of course, the left side). I would unplug the throat mike and move to a position where the pilot could see me through his window, and I would give a hand signal (or wands at night time) for him to taxi.

One night, about 23.30 hours, we went out to check the last Vulcan for hot brakes. I plugged in my headset and listened to the after-flight checks coming over my headphones. It went something like this:

"Flaps central."

"Check."

"Landing lights off."

"Check."

"Navigation lights."

"Not on."

"What? We haven't been flying without navigation lights, have we? We could have collided with someone else up there!"

"I doubt that, sir, there's no one else flying at this time of night. Only us silly buggers!"

We did the fire checks on the aircraft and cleared it to taxi to the dispersal. Later the following week, the crew of that Vulcan came into the crash bay restroom with *The Scampton Times* in their hands, demanding to know who 'Coggy' was. I had put the conversation in the 'Overheard' column of the station newspaper. It was a bit of good humour and the aircrew loved it. After that, whenever flying finished for the day or night, the aircrew would give us fire crew what they had left of their flying rations: sandwiches chocolate and sweets etc.

As well as crash crew duties, we had to provide domestic fire coverage for the station in general and would get frequent call outs to chimney fires, domestic cooker fires, and occasionally larger fires. In the event of a larger fire, we were always a 'first in line' service; as soon as the civil fire brigade turned up, they took over command. Aircraft and crash fires were usually our call, because of our specialist skills and equipment used for those purposes. Although the civil fire brigade had the authority to take over any major fire, be it domestic or aircraft, with the latter they usually let us deal with it.

During a non-flying weekend whilst on duty in charge of the domestic crew, one of our firemen coming on duty noticed a lot of smoke coming from a barn on the farm over the road from the camp. I phoned the duty officer to ask if I could investigate. Having got permission, I took the Land Rover and the domestic tender to the farm. The remainder of the crew stayed in the crash bays to give cover to aircraft on the dispersals.

On arrival at the farm, we were met by a frantic farmer waving and shouting for us to save his barn and combine harvester, which was also parked in the barn. The fire was by now burning fiercely, so I directed the domestic water tender to apply water spray to the seat of the fire, which was in fact bales of straw. Meanwhile, I had left instructions before I left camp for one of the crew that was left there to call Lincoln Fire Brigade. The other crew members were laying out hoses from the nearest hydrant, approximately 100 yards away, which kept our water tender replenished.

The civilian fire brigade arrived soon after we had the fire under control, and I informed the sub officer in charge of what we had already achieved. He took over responsibility but asked if our hoses from the hydrant could be coupled to his tender to keep it replenished so he could douse down the embers. He said he would come over to the crash bays to bring our hoses back and asked if we could "get the kettle on!"

Later that year, my daughter had a couple of tame rabbits in a hutch in our back garden. I went over to the farm, introduced myself to the farmer and asked if he remembered me. He didn't, so I told him I had saved his barn and combine harvester. He was very appreciative and thanked me. However, when I asked if I could buy half a bale of straw for my daughter's rabbits, he said, "Yes, of course," and only charged me a pound instead of the usual two pounds. Talk to me about how tight farmers are...!

Another rather odd incident occurred sometime later. It was on a very misty morning on the grass area separating our crash bays and the runway. I was filling in the occurrence log when one of the other lads in our crew saw someone walking across the grass in front of our office window. I took a couple of the guys and we armed ourselves with small crowbars. We shouted for the stranger to stop and challenged him to show his identity. Having got closer, we realised it was the station commander. After we had apologised, he commended us on our vigilance and said we had done everything he would have expected anyone on the station to do. "One cannot just wander anywhere on a military establishment without permission," he said. He mentioned he'd had to reprimand a dog handler who was guarding one of the dispersals because he hadn't been challenged.

I received my Long Service and Good Conduct medals in my eighteenth year of service. Present at the ceremony to mark the occasion was the station commander who had just taken over the station and seven chief technicians and warrant officers. Not unexpectedly, I was awarded my medals last, being the lowest in rank. I won't mention the commanding officer's name, but on my turn to be awarded my medal he made a speech.

"Corporal Coggon has been last to receive his medal for a very good reason," he said, "and that is that whilst in Singapore at RAF Tengah in 1966, Corporal Coggon most definitely saved me from serious injury, when, with disregard for his own safety, he got me out of a smoke-filled Canberra cockpit where I had become semi-conscious from the inhalation of smoke fumes from electrical wiring and was not able to use oxygen for fear of starting a rapid combustion. Now, whilst not taking anything away from the rest of you gentlemen, I proudly congratulate Coggon and thank him."

He congratulated us all and we all took his toast with a glass of wine each. I was pleasantly surprised by his words.

While I was at Scampton I took a correspondence course for the second year of a City and Guilds in radio and television servicing. I also took the Radio Amateurs course, which is also a City and Guilds examination. My good friend Les, whose surname I will not mention in case he objects, helped me with the practical side of electronics and their applications. He worked in the ground radio servicing section in the base of the control tower next door to the crash bays, and it was convenient for me to go over there and do a fair bit of repair work under his supervision. For all those radio amateurs out there, our call signs were initially G8LGK, my call and his G8JIC, but we later passed our Morse test and so became class A licensees, mine being G4FYE.

One night, after flying finished, I was last to leave as it was my turn to turn off the airfield lighting on the runway and perimeter tracks. Then I had to cycle to my married quarter along the darkened perimeter track. I remember riding along, whistling, and without any lights on my cycle. Suddenly there was a terrific clatter as I collided with another cyclist without lights. Bearing in mind that the perimeter track is at least fifty metres wide, the chance of us colliding was about a thousand to one! We were both unhurt, but our RAF service bicycles were quite buckled. We sat there laughing our heads off at each other.

CHAPTER NINETEEN

In 1975 I was detached to RAF St Athens in South Wales for my Mk V1 course. This involved three weeks' road and cross country driving of an advanced fire tender, capable of speeds up to 40 mile per hour over rough moorland and through four feet of water.

To complete the test of competence to drive this vehicle we had to negotiate a dirt road that ran into a quarry, where the road track went under water about four feet deep for fifty yards. Then we went up onto an island in the middle of the quarry and exited the other side by a similar track under water. On either side of the track there were channels of water to a depth of seventy feet. Bear in mind, that, when hitting the water at a speed of about 30 miles per hour, you're driving blind because the water comes over the top of the vehicle in a bow wave. The only indicators were three black and white marker posts you had to keep in line.

After this course I did the post graduate Senior Man Management and Instructional Technique course at the School of Education at RAF Upton and also the Heavy Rescue course at RAF Catterick. In fact, even though I was still a corporal I was qualified to the rank of warrant officer. However, it was one of those trades that required more Indians than chiefs, and there were not enough vacancies for chiefs.

During the 1977 fire strike I was sent to Northern Ireland as a commander of a Green Goddess crew but was later selected as part of a specialist breathing apparatus team. We worked in smoke-filled buildings using Siebre Gorman breathing apparatus, the cylinders each holding 2000lb per square inch of compressed air pressure. (Later, when I was back at Scampton, I trained to use the prototype that recycled exhaled air and made more oxygen.)

We were based and billeted at Fort George in Londonderry and experienced many incidents where we were spat at and called names – even when we were saving lives. One day, another breathing apparatus operator and I went into a house whose occupants were reluctant to let us in for fear of reprisals from their neighbours, who were throwing stones at us. Some people were encouraging us to go in and find a missing fourteen-year-old boy and others were trying to stop us. We ignored the protests and barged through the door and up the stairs to the landing. The house was filling with smoke that appeared to be coming from the attic. Eventually we extinguished it using a spray nozzle and first aid hose reel from the Green Goddess. I found the boy in the attic of the house next door; he had crawled through before succumbing to the smoke. I put the spare face mask on him and turned on the air pressure and he responded almost immediately, coughing and spluttering but struggling to get away as we pulled him back down the stairs. Apparently, this youth had in fact set fire to his neighbour's attic; he and they were of different religions and were always having a go at each other.

Most of the terraced houses had escape routes for the IRA, passageways cut through the brickwork to allow them to travel through to adjoining attics. People who opposed the IRA were threatened with reprisals if they mentioned the escape routes to the police. This was, of course, during the time of The Troubles and we were being protected by armed soldiers of the Black Watch and the Grenadier Guards. I have to say, though, that in most areas of Northern Ireland the people as a whole were good, honest, hard-working folk, and it was spoilt by a minority of radicals who held a grudge for a century or more.

The next emergency was a fire bomb in a factory. We were parked in a Land Rover outside the building next door, which was also was a factory, waiting while the radio-controlled robot camera was steered around the burning building looking for more bombs. We were all kitted up with breathing apparatus cylinders on our backs, waiting in case there was need for a rescue.

What we weren't ready for was the ear-shattering explosion that took our Land Rover up off its wheels and thumped us back down onto the road again – landing back on its wheels, luckily for us. I hate to think what a mess we would have been if those 2000lbs per square inch cylinders of pressurised air had ruptured.

A bomb had been placed in the building we were parked outside specifically to blow up any rescue military who may be looking for more explosive devices in the area.

Another time we were asked to help extinguish a large shop fire. I was standing on a ladder, fighting the fire by aiming the water jet at the roof top, when I was pulled down off the ladder by a soldier who was tugging at my trouser legs to get my attention. I gave the hand signal to the pump operator to cut the water and climbed down the ladder. We were hurried into cover and I was told that a sniper was firing at us. Later, I was shown the bullet hole, which went right through the aluminium ladder just below where I had been standing. The building was left to burn out, as it was too dangerous for us to continue trying to fight the blaze with the added danger of being shot at.

One soldier stationed at Fort George was shot dead while we were there, although I didn't see it myself. The soldier was walking back to his billet after having dinner in the mess and fell to the ground dead after being shot twice by a sniper apparently hiding in a local church tower. This particular sniper had been killing soldiers for some time now, we were told. He was hunted down, but somehow never caught, probably because the IRA were shielded by women and children, often by hiding them in a crowd.

I saw this at first hand whilst attending a fire. The gathered crowd suddenly parted, revealing two balaclava-clad men manning a machine gun. We only got a glimpse before the crowd closed their ranks again to hide the IRA men, who were doing this as a show of strength. They taunted our guards to fire on them, because if we killed anyone in the crowd it would enable the IRA to get sympathy and support from the press. That put the wind up me; we would have been sitting ducks to a machine gun that close. After that incident I was always more wary and, to be honest, scared when I was idle; when busy, you hadn't time to be scared.

During the Christmas Day shift we were billeted in a garage where we were watching a TV that the army had brought in. The lads had been given one can of beer each. In the semi-darkness of the room, halfway through a film one of our guardsmen screamed and started swearing very loudly, protesting that one of his mates had stabbed his leg with a dinner fork. Being the NCO in charge, I switched the lights on and discovered that a Black Watch soldier was the perpetrator of the stabbing, which had obviously been done with vicious intent by the look of the nasty wound on the other man's leg. I asked what the hell was going on and was instantly aware that the soldier who had inflicted the injury had a half bottle of whisky in his hand and was as drunk as a drunk can be.

Because of the severity of the injury, I could not let this go unpunished. I told this lad I was charging him with being drunk on duty, and unlawfully wounding another soldier.

He got up and went into the bedroom, I thought to get his coat, but he came back with a rifle. After loading it, he pointed the weapon at my stomach. I froze. This was super serious, and I was at a loss for what to do. If I in any way retaliated, he would shoot me; if I said anything, he may have shot me. The lad he had stabbed was the last person I thought would come to my rescue, but he grabbed the muzzle of the rifle, pulled it away from my stomach and pressed it into his own. In my opinion, he was a hero.

Then he said to his mate, calmly, "If you are going to shoot anyone, it will be me, so go ahead and do it, or give me the f-----g rifle."

The guy just let go of the rifle and was marched out of the building to the guardroom, escorted by his own mates.

Later that year I had to attend a court martial and the soldier was sent to Colchester Army Correction Centre.

CHAPTER TWENTY

The flight back to RAF Scampton didn't take very long and everyone was talking about what they had done in the fire brigades during the strike. I didn't say a lot, but my experience of it was hairy, to say the least. Still, it was an experience I would never forget. When someone who's drunk puts a loaded SLR with the barrel touching your belly button, how could anyone forget that in a hurry?

In my last year at RAF Scampton we had a new sergeant in charge of our crew. Now, I am not one to encourage bad behaviour, but this sergeant was always trying to pull jokes at other people's expense. Some of the things he did were childish, like sending one of the young new lads to the station workshop to borrow a left-handed saw or sending a young airman to the paint finishing shop to ask for a gallon of striped paint. I know, it sounds petty, and it was. Anyway, I won't say who was responsible for the retaliation that was played on this particular sergeant, but I don't deny seeding the idea.

One of our duties was to service and inspect fire extinguishers, and one extinguisher in particular was known as the 'two-gallon foam'. To service the extinguisher, one had to mix one and a half gallons of water with a sachet of powder that contained bicarbonate of soda and liquorish, which turned dark brown when mixed with the water. This was then put into the outer container of the extinguisher. The inner metal container contained a quart of water and a sachet of aluminium sulphate, which when mixed with water is colourless. It was then poured into the inner container, which in turn was placed carefully into the outer container with a loose lead sealing ball in a cradle at the top of the quart cylinder. To set off the extinguisher, one tipped it upside down, held a finger over the nozzle and gave it a good shake. This enabled the lead ball to come away from the seal of the inner container and mix with the outer cylinder contents. This action caused the two chemicals, when mixed, to produce carbon dioxide-filled bubbles, which of course was the foam. The liquorish was added to make it adhere to whatever it came into contact with. The expansion ratio of the two-gallon foam extinguisher was eight to one, meaning it created 16 gallons of foam.

I won't say who put the sachet of bicarbonate of soda and liquorish in the cistern, and the clear solution of aluminium sulphate in the bowl of the SNCO's toilet, but I can say that eight gallons of very sticky foam almost covered its intended victim.

CHAPTER TWENTY-ONE

On 24th November 1978 – my 40th birthday – my military service of 22 years ended. I was asked to sign on for another 15 years, but I declined. My children were by now doing their exams and I thought it would be difficult to get another job if I waited until I was 55. So, I took my gratuity and my allotted pension and was demobbed. We did not vacate our married quarter straight away, though; we were waiting for a council house in Doncaster, where we had been on the list for a number of years.

Three weeks after my demob, I got a job at Radio Rentals in Lincoln, repairing televisions. I enjoyed the job, but the wages were low considering I had to spend one day a week unpaid at Lincoln Technical College, being updated on the new technology of semiconductors that were replacing valve circuitry. The other downside to the job was having to carry heavy hybrid televisions up and down flights of stairs when I had to take a set back to the workshop to do the repair. We were also expected to use our own transport for a minimum mileage allowance. Anyway, after six months, we were offered a council house in Doncaster and I gave in my notice.

My intention was to look for a similar job in Doncaster but while I was looking in the job centre I saw a better paid option, and I got a job with South Yorkshire Transport Executive as a bus driver. The wages were far better and as I already had a PSV licence I only needed training on the ticket machines and the different routes. That turned out to be a laugh, because we new drivers were taken out to learn the routes in an enclosed van with no side windows. When the training finished and you were put on service you were lucky to have a 'clippie' (conductress) who told you the route until you knew it. Otherwise, you waited for the passengers' cry of, "Hey, he's going the wrong way!" Then you mentioned that you were a new driver, and asked, "Which way is it then?" One soon got to know all the routes – and there were many.

We worked shifts, and the day shift started around 04.00 hours. The first job would be to book the bus out of the depot and then go to the surrounding villages to collect the miners and take them to the many pits in the borough. That done, we would again go around the villages to collect the factory workers; we took workers to Pilkington Glass, International Harvesters, Pegler Taps, Imperial Chemical Industry, Crompton Light Bulbs and British Wire Ropes, to name a few. We would then take school children to several different schools in and around Doncaster. By around 09.00 hours you would be on normal passenger service. Some of us would be driving these workers and school runs as overtime and then starting our normal shifts at around 1400 hours until midnight. It would also work like that at evening time: if you had started the early morning shift you got compulsory overtime to take the workers home again after you had finished your normal day's work on passenger service.

At that time in 1979 fares were only a few pence. Passengers could travel twenty miles to Sheffield from

Doncaster for two shillings and sixpence or get to practically any urban area of Doncaster for seven pennies. Pensioners travelled free with their pension passes in off peak time, which was from 9am to 10pm during the week; there was no time limit on the weekends and bank holidays.

Later, we were trained to operate one-person buses, where the driver collected the fares from the driving seat. The clippies were phased out, retrained as drivers or transferred to the disabled vehicles that required attendants for wheelchair passengers.

I remember one particular incident. I was driving the last bus from town on route to Edlington, a mining suburb of Doncaster. I was driving on Balby Road when I got a radio message from our bus depot saying that someone had been pushed out of the rear window – the emergency escape exit – on the upper deck of the double decker bus I was driving. The person seemed to be uninjured as he got up off the road and ran off, but I was asked to investigate what was going on. So, after parking in a bus stop, I went up onto the top deck. A group of miners told me that the man who fell out of the window was ripping up the seats with a knife. They showed me the rear seat, which was cut to pieces. They told him to pack it in, but he carried on wilfully damaging the seats. I asked them how he had ended up out of the window. Some of them just laughed, and one said, "He forgot to ring the bell."

The police turned up but when they heard the story nothing could be done as there wasn't enough evidence. We all knew the truth though. Miners always looked after us bus drivers, and we used to go around Edlington village twice with the last bus at the weekend, unofficially, to get them all home from the miners' clubs.

On another occasion, I went to pick up school kids from a school that many in our town will remember being nicknamed 'Grange Hill', after the television series about an unruly school. On route to their destination, the kids on the upper deck almost caused a major disaster by all moving at once from one side of the upper deck to other, making the bus tip from side to side and deliberately making it swerve. Luckily, I managed to slow the vehicle to a stop quickly but even whilst it was stationary, they were still moving from side to side, en masse, to frighten those kids who were not involved. Some motorists who had been behind the bus and witnessed what the kids had been doing stopped, the police turned up, and the instigators were sorted out.

My first marriage ended in divorce after 27 years. Our relationship had just drifted apart over the years and I blame myself, because of the many times I had to go away from my family while I was in the forces. It wasn't much of a life for Christine, left to look after three children on her own most of the time. We had paid a mortgage on the council house and came to an agreement. I left the house and all contents to Christine and my children, and I kept my RAF pension. Approximately two years after our divorce we both remarried new partners. By then, my children had all left school and were married themselves.

I continued to work on the buses for 19 years. The company offered me early retirement when they brought in new drivers to work on minibuses and cut down the routes operated by double deckers. This came with an attractive pension, so I took it.

A Day with a Yorkshire Bus Driver

'A twentyfive an' eres me pass,
En one fo't' daughter ent t'other lass.'
'Yer carn't use tha pass, tisn't time,
Tha'll hav to wait till hafe past nine.'
'Mornin driver, fifty if ya please,'
The old man said with a wheeze.
'Hey up there mate, ta very much,'
As he jerked sharply with the clutch.
Ding! 'Next stop, lad, if yer please,
Just round t' corner past them trees.'
'Keep set darn wi all tha shoppin,
Or tha'll tipple ower whilst bus is stoppin'.'
'Tickets please,' The bus inspector said.
'Av lost mine, luv,' said a woman, going red.
'Where t' board, lass?' 'Tiller lane.'
'Well gerrit fon, or tha pays again.'
'Steady on, tha'll hev me ower,
An nar thas trapped me in tha door.'
'Awe gi' up meckin such a fuss,
It's tha own fault, don't blame us.'
'How much fot two baines en me?'
'Depends, where's tha goin?' said he.
'We'er oft to me mam's,' she replied.
'Gi us a clue lass, where's that? he sighed.
Ten past, half past, on the hour,
enough to make any driver sour.
Wow! Last bus soon, eleven o'clock,
then am off home ter me bed, old cock.

G F COGGON, 1994

CHAPTER TWENTY-TWO

Mary and I were married at Doncaster register office and together we bought the council house she lived in with her grown-up children. A week after leaving the buses, I got a job long distance lorry driving for a transport firm not far away in Blaxton.

The job was delivering glass for shop windows, aquariums and the like. It was picked up from Hull Docks and transported all over the British Isles. On my lorry, which was an eight-wheeler Volvo, my sleeper cab was above my driving cab, forming a sort of double decker cab. Also on the vehicle was a crane, which I had been trained to operate. I had the appropriate certificate of competence; this and a site safety certificate were required by law.

After two years I went on a three-week Heavy Goods One course in Leeds and passed the test. Back at my company, I was given charge of a brand-new walk-through DAF tractor unit and trailer with a ride-on crane, and I delivered building supplies, bricks, concrete blocks and, later, concrete reinforced floor beams. It meant setting off on a Monday morning, having loaded late afternoon on the previous Friday, then staying out on the road until the following Friday. A typical example would be to drop off in London somewhere on a building site, then go to the nearest place where you could pick up another load, usually near Oxford. Then you drove as far as possible towards your next drop before you had to stop the night at a truck stop because you were limited by your tachometer on the hours you could drive. The law stated that you put a disk chart in the tachometer, and it recorded everything you did with the truck – all the actual driving movements and stops. Normally, by law you could only drive for four hours before taking a forty-five-minute break, where you had to switch off your engine. Then you could drive for another four hours, after which followed an eight-hour rest period. On two occasions in a week, you could drive a nine-hour shift as opposed to the normal eight hour one. (A year before I retired, the chart system was changed to a plastic tachograph record card.)

Sometimes if I got close to the depot I would come home for the night. However, my tractor unit had all mod cons, including an oven, fridge, bunk bed, television and night heaters. So what I used to do – like many other drivers – was go into the nearest truck stop and have my ablutions, then drive back onto the highway and find a nice secluded layby or a factory site where I could park up, cook my own meal and watch television. If I didn't feel like cooking, I would pay for parking in a truck stop (reimbursable by the firm) and buy a hot meal instead.

Safety equipment was also necessary and when entering a building site, I had to be wearing a yellow reflective jacket, hard hat, goggles and safety boots. If you were minus any of these items, you would be refused to deliver at the site.

This was initially a good rule, but in due course, safety equipment laws became silly. For instance, if it was raining while you were twelve feet up on your crane seat lifting the floor beams (sometimes up to a ton of concrete beams at a time), your goggles would steam up or become that peppered with rain that it was impossible to see through them, so putting the guy who was laying down skid wood to stack the beams on in danger of being crushed or trapped by the swinging manoeuvring beams in the crane grab.

I remember going to central London one day, all the way from Featherstone in West Yorkshire, where we mostly collected our loads of floor beams. I arrived on the site and was about to start unloading when the site foreman came along with a safety inspector. I was asked if I possessed a safety belt to wear on the crane seat, which is about twelve feet above the ground. When I answered that none of us crane drivers had ever been required to wear a safety belt, nor was there any fitted on the crane control seat, he said I could not unload. "Fine," I answered, "I'll get the load strapped up and take them back to Featherstone."

These beams were tailor-made to fit the plots they were intended for and could not be used on other sites; they would simply not fit. I had just finished putting the tie straps back around the beams when the site foreman came running over to me and asked me if I would wait a few minutes because the safety officer had agreed a solution. Five minutes later, a fork lift brought two one-tonne bags filled with polystyrene pellets, which they placed around the base of my crane tower in case I fell off.

A few years later, I was using another older trailer that had a very old type of crane, and if on that occasion I had been wearing a seat belt, I certainly would not be here now writing this story. Halfway through unloading, craning off some very large heavy floor beams and working to the safety limit of the crane, I felt a sudden lurch and heard a sharp metallic crack as the crane tower started to bend. I immediately knew what was happening and jumped the twelve feet to the ground, just as the crane and the beams crashed down over the side of the trailer. I was very, very lucky. If I had been delayed by having to undo a safety belt it most likely would have been a different story.

I remember parking in a layby one night on the A13 (a dual carriageway into London), just under the M25 at Dartford Bridge. I awoke the following morning to discover that my diesel tanks had been siphoned out during the night. To this day I cannot imagine how someone would have the nerve to siphon fuel on a busy road such as the A13. My boss contacted the insurance people and brought me enough diesel to get me to a garage.

My dear wife Mary – or Ida-Mary, as she is sometimes called by her brothers and sisters – came over from Ireland with her family when she was only eight years old. She worked as a cleaner when we got married and sometimes, when not working, came with me on my journeys around the country.

Once we parked in a secluded layby near Silverstone on the A43. I was woken when the driver of the articulated curtain-sided truck in front of mine banged on my door. During the night someone had completely emptied his trailer and stolen 200 baby car seats. He asked me if I had heard anything, but neither of us had heard a thing.

I recall one occasion when we stopped overnight in a favourite place I had used several times before in Bedfordshire. I parked in the layby, which was alongside a very high wall. It was dark and there was hardly any traffic on the road. Mary got out of the cab to go on a private excursion but after a short time I heard a huge roar and poor Mary came running back, petrified. I had forgotten to tell her that on the other side of the wall was the lion park at Longleat Zoo! Anyway, we always enjoyed each other's company, and this was only one of the many trips we made together when she had time off from her work.

This was my tractor unit with a drop and go trailer, which could be shortened in length when the back part was empty by reversing the front part of the trailer on top of the rear section. This enabled me to get into smaller sites. The crane was a ride along the trailer, on tracks. The load on the trailer is floor beams; I carried up to 45 tons of reinforced concrete beams.

CHAPTER TWENTY-THREE

Between us, Mary and I had seven children. Whether they were Mary's children or my children, they have all been like my own flesh and blood.

My stepson Andrew studied at the University of Hull for a degree and Sonia, my stepdaughter, had also gained a degree from the University of Huddersfield and became a teacher in that city.

Scott, my other stepson, found work as a manager of a pylon servicing team on the National Grid; he and his team string the wires on pylons all over the country and he was even sent to Manila in the Philippines to tutor teams over there for a while. He married Helen and they now live nearby and have given us Alex and Emily, our dear grandchildren.

My son John and his wife Elaina went to live near Colditz in Germany. Claudia, my granddaughter-in-law, lives over here somewhere in Yorkshire, and my grandsons Michael and Shaun are also in Yorkshire.

My eldest daughter, Angela is at present off the radar. I have not seen her for ten years or more, and would love her to get in touch with me just to let me know that she and my grandchildren Lucy and Ben are all right. That would be nice.

My youngest daughter Joanne and her husband Simon

have five children: my three beautiful granddaughters Jodey, Leah and Milly, and my grandsons Scott and Bradley. Bradley is studying for a degree at the University of Essex. They all live quite close to Mary and me and we are in close contact.

We also have Mary's eldest son Stephen and his wife Jodie, who live in Doncaster with our grandsons Kurt and Aaron and granddaughter Janelle, who in turn has provided us with a beautiful little great granddaughter, Lunar.

While I was working on the lorries, I found out that I had prostate cancer. This came as a great shock because although I was feeling washed out by the end of a shift working with concrete, I thought it was me just getting a bit long in the tooth. However, after a blood test I was sent to Barnsley Hospital for a biopsy of my prostate gland and was found to have an extensive cancer of the prostate.

My boss allowed me to stay on at work part time while I travelled to and from Sheffield every day for three months of radiotherapy treatment. I would work mornings and go for treatment in the afternoon, then come back to work for a couple of hours at night. It was very good of my employer to allow me to do this because Mary and I had to keep a wage coming in to pay the mortgage.

The treatment took about an hour, but the longest part was travelling to and from the hospital at Sheffield. I had to drink a quart of water before lying very still on the bed while the machine fired radiation at the cancer. Drinking the water prevented the radiation from going through my bladder into other parts of my body, but the pressure on my bladder became almost unbearable with all that water inside me. Mary always came with me, bless her, and she wasn't exactly a well woman herself, as she has no thyroid gland and has to take the drug thyroxine. Anyway, I finished the treatment, and I am now 12 years in remission and, fingers crossed, clear.

Ever since I left the RAF I have made many friends who gave me support during this worrying time, and I would like to mention a couple of them here: Stewart Piper and his wife Katherine, who always helped me with transport if I was stuck; and my manager Mike Smith, who made things work for us financially by keeping me in work, albeit only on light duties. Of course, my family have always been there for me. Finally, I need to thank my dearest Mary, my soulmate. But for her, I would have given up.

I retired at seventy-one, mainly because the insurance to keep me working on a crane was expensive from my boss's point of view, but mostly because I had developed Type 2 Diabetes by then.

Just after I retired, our son – my stepson Andrew, who I have always loved and admired – was killed in a road accident whilst out riding his bicycle. Andrew was a safety officer with UNISON, and he visited hospitals teaching health and safety. He was also a competent cyclist and a member of the Doncaster Wheelers Cycling Club. He was so safety conscious, especially when it came to road safety, and his death came as a shock to us all. It devastated us, especially poor Mary, who was heartbroken, as any mother would be. However, Mary is also a victim of Parkinson's disease and the loss of our dear son has made her illness worse.

Me with my grandson Alex on his first driving lesson

My wife Mary

The Highway of Life

Life is like a philosophical roundabout
With a million roads of hidden doubt,
Through viaducts of our hidden mind,
Along highways to our future find.
Suspended in our bridge of thought
The right of way to our destiny sought.
Frequently lost in some dark alley
Where thought and concentration rally.
Curiosity speeds us around the bend
And finds the beginning of the end.
The tunnel of life predicts our fate,
Paying our fine at the last tollgate.

G F COGGON, 1994

CHAPTER TWENTY-FOUR

Despite having Parkinson's disease and other health problems, my dear wife Mary continues to keep going. She is an inspiration to anyone who is crippled with this terrible disease. Mary is the kindest, most unselfish person I have ever met in my 82 years and I love her more than I could write words to express. She has looked after me and others, putting our needs before her own, and I make no excuse for telling everyone who reads my book.

At the time of writing, we are now in the middle of something I never thought I would witness in my lifetime: a pandemic of great magnitude, causing enormous rates of death and suffering around the world. The coronavirus COVID-19 has the potential to changes the lives of survivors forever.

I have had a few near misses in life, but I have had many adventures that I hope you have enjoyed sharing with me by reading my story.

Age has suddenly caught up with me but, like my dear wife Mary, I am determined to keep going. I would very much like us both to receive that famous birthday card from Buckingham Palace to celebrate 100 years.

However, don't ever think that life stops when you retire.

I very often thought, "I wish I was still working," but as time went on, I found so much to do that I could not find enough time to do it all.

I have always liked birds and I found a lot of joy making wooden bird houses and feeders. I still feed the birds and draw them and make other wooden garden ornaments and household gadgets. One of the things I make is garden windmills and I use the axles from bicycle wheels to pivot the sails.

As a doctor once told me, do all your active sport before you reach fifty but make sure you still get plenty of exercise by walking or gardening. When I was younger, I was always very active, playing football, volleyball, badminton or squash, and I think that has enabled me to reach my present age of 82 with a reasonable amount of fitness, even though I have the usual old age complaints such as deafness and cataracts. Actually, I have just had one cataract removed, and my sight is normal again; this is essential for me as I still drive.

I mentioned earlier that I was a licensed radio amateur, this is of course another outlet for not getting bored, although I am not so active now as I used to be. I can still read Morse by sound, up to twenty words per minute, which, incidentally, was part of my exam to become an amateur radio operator. The exam is the two-year City and Guilds in electronics and radio circuitry, which enables one to get the 'B' licence and use short distance radio (VHF: very high frequency). To get the 'A' licence (SW – short wave) I had to take a twelve word per minute Morse test at the Royal Naval Establishment at Trusthorpe, on the east coast. This mode of radio is bounced off the troposphere with suitable aerials. It's pretty much like the old CB radio but more involved, because we also do amateur television, RITTY and satellite radio.

Another of my hobbies is art. I paint and draw, mostly in oils or pastels but I have also used pen and ink or watercolour. I have written lots of poems but so far have not published a book of them – but I've had some published in other people's books. You can see a few of my paintings at the end of the book, and you'll have read some of my poems already.

So, you can see I keep myself very busy. I think that is the way to enjoy life to the full.

*My amateur radio station (G4FYE), which I share with another
amateur, my Mary, who is also a 'B' licensed amateur radio
operator (M3HOX).*

CHAPTER TWENTY-FIVE

Retirement also gave me the time to join the British Nuclear Test Veterans Association and work with them to try and get justice for all the men who died young through no fault of their own. They didn't ask to be guinea pigs or to be bombarded with radiation in the 1950s and 1960s. They were ordered to carry out duties that were extremely dangerous, not only to the veterans themselves but also to their children and their children's children.

When taken into your body via breathing, the mouth or a wound, alpha particles can and do destroy blood cells; they can be in your body for a lifetime before you see the damage. It has been 60-odd years since the hydrogen bomb tests and still the British Government denies any radiation was present. The BNTVA has been fighting for compensation and a medal for the veterans for over half a century. They have given the Ministry of Defence (MOD) proof of the radiation fallout at those tests through the countless illnesses and deaths of the participants. The MOD has denied there was any radiation. However, every other superpower government that carried out atomic tests has recognised the harm they brought on their troops during these tests and given them compensation and a medal, therefore recognising the health problems they have brought onto these men and their families.

I was made to wash a Canberra aircraft that had flown through the hydrogen bomb cloud. I wore only a pair of denims, gloves and wellingtons and a cotton face mask – no other protection. I then scrubbed myself for two and a half hours in the decontamination showers before the Geiger counter stopped registering radiation on the outside of my body. But what about what I may have swallowed? Alpha particles cannot penetrate skin, so they remain trapped inside your body for years if you swallow or breath them in.

For half a century we have been unable to say anything about what happened. But now, because of the Freedom of Speech Act and with the release of information that was kept under the Official Secrets Act for fifty years, our voice is being heard across the world.

LABRATS is an organisation that is helping to spread the news – but sadly not before most of those who witnessed the British nuclear tests have passed.

I was 82 on 24th November 2020 and, like so many of my fellow lab rats/guinea pigs, I have never been recognised for my part in the tests.

This book, and the one I wrote before it (an e-book on Kindle*) is my contribution to our 70-year appeal to the British Government to recognise the hardships many of us have suffered.

Christmas Island 1957-1958 by Gordon Frederick Coggon

Spidery contrails mark the sky above the Pacific five miles high.

Two Valiant bombers wing their way over Christmas Island's coral bay.

Three thousand troops sit and wait, amongs't the trees not knowing their fate.

Loud speakers all around them sound their relayed message from air to ground.

'Final countdown.' 'One minute,' they say. 'Sit behind a tree and face away.

'Put your beret over your eyes and push your head between your thighs.

'Ninety-eight, ninety-seven, ninety-six ... all systems go for the final fix.'

Three thousand guinea pigs are we, not knowing if tomorrow will be.

'Ground zero! Bomb gone! Aircraft away! Cover your eyes until I say.'

Silent seconds ticking past, no big bang, no crash or blast.

Then, suddenly, nightmare in the sands, through my beret, my bones, my hands.

Intense heat, creeping slow ... through my body, no burns to show.

Panic! I take a look, nothing in sight, nothing at all, but blinding white.

I tell myself, everything's OK; X-ray? Heat? ... It was the Gamma ray.

A minute passes. The tannoys sound. 'You can stand up now

and turn around.'

There ... half the horizon, half the sky, filled with a mushroom ten miles high!

Like a huge sun changing colour, growing, expanding, getting fuller.

A stem of water, a half mile wide, thirsty sucked from the ocean's tide.

A minute later we watched in awe, travelling outward from the core

A beautiful halo leaving clear blue sky, vaporising clouds in its path that lie.

Watching the halo pass overhead brought a great noise! A terrible dread.

A hurricane wind of strength so high it threw us about. Frightened, we cry.

Many were hurt, many now dead, to benefit the future of mankind, they said.

Radiation, it's a killer of men, caused by uranium, plutonium and hydrogen.

G F COGGON, 1980

Over the years I have done many oil paintings. Some I have kept, but most of them have been given to friends or sold. Here are a few of my favourites.

A day at Bridlington with my grandson Alex.
G F COGGON, 2012

Waterfowl on Cantley Park in Doncaster. G F COGGON, 2011

These two paintings of meerkats were inspired by a visit to The Yorkshire Wildlife Park, also situated near my home in Doncaster.
G F COGGON, 2014

I completed this painting after a trip into the Highlands of Scotland.
G.F.COGGON, 2013

ACKNOWLEDGEMENTS

I would like to thank my family and friends who have always encouraged me in my hobbies, especially my lovely wife, Mary.

Thank you also to my neighbour and friend Dave Faulding, who has helped me with some home electrical tasks and did a proofreading of this book for me.

A special thank you to Alan Owen, the founder of LABRATS, who has helped many veterans throughout the world by uniting them in their cause for justice against some governments who still after seventy years have not given nuclear veterans any recognition. The BNTVA (The British Nuclear Test Veterans Association) has been campaigning on our behalf for seventy-odd years now, and still the Government denies any harm was done to the guinea pigs they used during the tests. Most of the nuclear powers of the world have recognised their veterans by compensating them, and/or awarding medals, and so honouring the important part they undertook in the experiments they were ordered to carry out, thereby exposing themselves to toxic radiation.

My thanks also to Helen Watson, my daughter-in-law, for her valuable help in editing this book.

Finally, I'd like to thank Alison Thompson, The Proof Fairy, for without her help this book may never have been published.

Printed in Great Britain
by Amazon

24688313R00071